MIND
OVER
MONEY

MIND
OVER
MONEY

Your Path to Wealth and Happiness

ERIC TYSON

c d s
BOOKS
New York

Published by CDS Books

Cataloging-in-Publication data for this book is available from the Library of Congress.

ISBN-13: 978-1-59315-238-3
ISBN-10: 1-59315-238-8

CDS books are available at special discounts for bulk purchases in the United States by corporations, institutions, and other organizations. For more information, please contact the Special Markets Department at the Perseus Books Group, 11 Cambridge Center, Cambridge, MA 02142; call (800) 255-1514 or (617) 252-5298; or e-mail special.markets@perseusbooks.com.

06 07 08 / 10 9 8 7 6 5 4 3 2 1

To my mom and dad who accomplished so much starting from so little, and to my former financial counseling clients and students for their courage to share their hard knocks and willingness to grow and learn from their mistakes.

CONTENTS

PREFACE

Just a generation ago, finding a television station that provided much more than a two-minute stock-market update was difficult. Today, we're bombarded with financial advice. Entire television networks, radio shows, magazines, and Web sites are devoted solely to this realm (not to mention all the company that I keep on bookstore shelves). With ready access to more information and advice than ever before, one might expect that managing investments, saving for retirement, getting out of debt, and taking care of a whole host of financial issues would be getting significantly easier for just about everyone. However, my experience has demonstrated that just the opposite is true. I've seen plenty of intelligent and well-intentioned people with access to all that information fail to master their personal finances.

These folks would find nothing to object to in the three principles that form my perspective on personal finance—you should spend less than you earn, you should regularly save toward future goals, and you should buy and hold solid investments with an eye toward the long term. In fact, most people already know the validity of these points. However, even with this knowledge in hand, tens of millions of people still haven't been able to overcome the financially detrimental behaviors preventing them from putting their knowledge into action and getting on the best financial path. Many aren't even consciously aware of these behaviors or that they're a problem.

Although, on occasion, a major illness or some other unavoidable problem causes people to fall short of their financial goals, far more often long-standing barriers to dealing well with money are to blame. As a financial counselor, I worked with many more people who had to overcome significant obstacles in their attitudes and behaviors than people who simply needed a bit of sound financial advice to implement. These impediments included spending temptations and casual acceptance of consumer debt, workaholism, letting greed or fear influence investing decisions, gambling and other addictive behaviors, hoarding tendencies, money avoidance and disorganization, and fighting about money within relationships. *Mind over Money* discusses these major financial obstacles to dealing with money that I've observed through my years of work as a financial counselor, lecturer, and writer. Breaking down the barriers to dealing well with money requires time, effort, and, most important, the right approach. Let me make it clear that I'm not a shrink, and I don't delve into the pop-psychology realm in this book. But I have worked on the front lines with real people struggling through personal financial obstacles that affect every aspect of their lives, and I've worked with them to successfully break down those barriers. Likewise, this practical book will help you *recognize* and then *conquer* bad financial habits and develop good ones. I offer proven solutions to stop self-defeating financial habits and get you on the right path.

Each of these barriers to sound money management has its own root causes, signs, symptoms, and solutions, but at least one underlying issue is also at work. Faced with a constant barrage of commercial pressures, we're forced to fight an uphill battle against a consumer culture that increasingly defines success in life as the ability to purchase more of everything—more car, more house, more entertainment, more services. Unless we're aware of these external pressures, in time, they can easily warp our own definitions of what it means to be successful. Don't get me wrong—financial success is important. However, a common denominator to overcoming many of these barriers is to reevaluate what success means to you. Too many people end up unhealthy, overstressed, and without significant financial resources despite their decades of long work hours. Are you giving sufficient attention to your family, personal life, happiness, values, and health? *Mind over Money* explains how a surprising minority of people are able to achieve their financial and personal goals. Although some of these people aren't among the most financially wealthy of individuals, they're happy with the *overall* gains they've made in their lives.

As a financial counselor and teacher to people of all economic means, I've gained a unique inside perspective on the personal financial struggles and issues that plague many people. I've been involved in the financial services industry for more than two decades, originally as a management consultant, and know how investment, insurance, and other financial companies design and market products to convince you to buy what they're selling so they can maximize their bottom lines. I share that perspective with you in the coming pages.

Best-seller lists are littered with personal-finance and self-improvement books. People are clearly interested in doing more with their money and improving their personal awareness and happiness. To date, however, there has been little integration of these two important fields. Only rarely do personal financial–planning books deal with the barriers holding back people from making wise financial moves. *Mind over Money* synthesizes the latest research regarding how people relate to and deal with money—and each other.

I hope you enjoy and benefit from our journey together.

A GOOD, LONG LOOK
IN THE MONEY MIRROR

The basics of good personal-financial practice—spending less than you earn, investing your savings in proven vehicles for the long term, and securing adequate insurance coverage—are relatively simple. Many people, however, are unable to follow these rules for the same reasons people can't follow a diet: it's difficult, and it can be emotionally taxing. I've written some of the most popular financial guides of the past decade, I've worked personally with clients as a financial counselor, and I've taught financial-management courses to large groups. Through these experiences, I've seen that many people are unable to do the right thing because good financial habits emerge only when the individual possesses the right mind-set about money. Many people allow their individual fears, biases, mistaken beliefs, past experiences, and other quirks and demons, along with external pressures from a consumer society permanently set on fast-forward, to color and sabotage their efforts to practice good financial habits.

Take Nancy, for example. When Nancy came to see me for financial advice, she was a medical professional earning about $60,000 annually. Single and in her late thirties, she rented a modest apartment and had a six-figure nest egg that came from savings and some inheritance. Eager to learn more about money, she read financial publications and attended seminars but confided in me that she still felt as if she never really understood "what's going on with money." I learned that her father had made her major financial decisions over the years but died a few years earlier, leaving her alone and with even more money to manage.

As Nancy described her work, she spoke confidently and without hesitation. When our conversation turned to money, however, her self-assured aura cracked as she nervously fidgeted in her chair and explained her unease. Although she desired to cut back on full-time work by her fifties, she disliked "risky investments." Making choices paralyzed her, and she kept her money invested in a bank account and some bonds that a broker sold to her and she didn't understand. Her lack of knowledge was further highlighted by the fact that the bonds were being called; she had no idea that such a thing could happen and wasn't even clear what it meant.

Like so many of the people who came to me for financial counseling, Nancy knew the importance of living within her means, making wise investments, and securing proper insurance. However, a number of barriers hampered her attempts to make sound financial decisions. The greatest obstacle was that Nancy was convinced that managing her money was beyond her capabilities. When she wrote down all the reasons why she couldn't make sound investing decisions, it became clear that many of her statements, and the beliefs that they reflected, came from what her father had told her over the years.

Just as significantly, Nancy was spending way too much time and energy consulting many different sources of financial advice. The cacophony created by all the talking heads and scribes overwhelmed and confused her, which reinforced her belief that she didn't know what she was doing. I put her on a financial news diet, an approach I advise many folks to take when they're on investment-information overload. We reviewed everything that she was reading and listening to and pared down the list by nearly 75 percent. Instead of plugging into the financial-news free-for-all, Nancy enrolled in the personal financial–management course that I used to teach at the University of California at Berkeley. In addition to reading quality investing books, she also performed various investment exercises and completed worksheets that steadily built her confidence and financial acumen while helping to deprogram the self-doubts she had accumulated through her father's influence. Nancy began investing a small portion of her money in highly diversified funds that included bonds and stocks to get her feet wet. She gained confidence with slightly riskier investments than she was used to, which allowed her money to grow.

Everyone Has Financial Faults

Nobody is a perfect financial manager. We all make money mistakes and face barriers to sound financial management. When I was attending college in 1980, inflation and interest rates were rocketing upward. I had saved money from summers spent working at my own landscaping company and decided to invest some of it in gold on the basis of advice I'd gleaned from some books in vogue at the time. (In retrospect, I would label such advice "doom and gloom.") I further made the error of trusting that a regular advertiser in the *Wall Street Journal*—the International Gold Bullion Exchange (IGBE)—was a legitimate company without doing further research. So I invested about $2,000 with the firm. To make a long story short, the Alderdice brothers who owned IGBE were ultimately arrested and imprisoned for defrauding investors. To add insult to injury, gold actually did well in the early 1980s. I simply shouldn't have bought the actual bullion and trusted that the company I bought it through would store (and secure) it for me. I learned some valuable (albeit costly) lessons from my foray into gold: check out the financial firms you do business with, never assume legitimacy on the basis of where a company promotes itself or is mentioned, and understand the risks of the specific investment vehicles you choose.

Commonly Reported Financial Blunders

In my work as a personal financial counselor, I had new clients complete a detailed questionnaire, which I then discussed with them in our first meeting. I was actually quite impressed with how many people completed this form and made our scheduled meeting without asking for more time. Completing the form required accessing many financial documents as well as reflecting on short- and long-term financial goals and concerns as well as financial decisions and issues that caused discomfort and displeasure. Of the hundreds of clients that I worked with over the years, all of them could point to mistakes.

Whether it's training airline pilots or paramedics, learning from (and avoiding) the mistakes of those who have come before you goes a long, long way toward doing your best at the endeavor at hand. Managing your money is no different. Here's a compilation of the prior mistakes that my clients routinely reported in their meetings with me. These same problems came up over and over again through the years. If you take these lessons to heart and commit to avoiding these errors, you can sidestep a lot of misery and lost money.

Failing to plan.   Some people continue to procrastinate and avoid thinking about and planning for their financial futures. One of the more common failures is not taking advantage of retirement plans offered by employers, including those offering free matching money. Think about recent vacations you've taken. You likely weighed some options in selecting a time and did some research to choose a destination, mode of transportation, accommodations, and so on. That vacation wouldn't have happened—and certainly wouldn't have turned out so well—without proper planning. Ditto for your future financial goals.

Using consumer credit.   Buying consumer goods (furniture, vacations, cars, dinners out—you name it) with credit cards and auto loans will cost you far more than you imagine in the long run. (Using a credit card for a transaction and then paying your bill in full when it's due is fine.) Besides getting you into the habit of spending money that you don't have, consumer credit usually comes with relatively high interest rates.

Leasing cars.   Many of my clients shared their regrets about leasing autos without understanding lease contracts, costs, and related issues. Extracting yourself from a lease takes enormous persistence and resolve, so it's better to avoid these expensive long-term car rentals in the first place.

Underestimating remodeling costs.   You've likely heard that construction inevitably takes longer and costs more than you expected up front. If your financial situation doesn't have much wiggle room and margin for error, sloppy planning can lead to unfinished projects and even personal bankruptcy.

Getting behind on taxes.   Although this error is more common among self-employed people, plenty of other folks fail to file their tax returns and pay the taxes they owe. In some cases, this situation results from a genuine problem understanding the tax system; in others, it's due to procrastination, denial, and lack of money.

Purchasing products sold by brokers.   Without a doubt, one of the biggest complaints I heard over the years from clients concerned investments they bought from brokers. Their dissatisfaction often stemmed from the fact that they bought these products without understanding the high fees and commissions associated with the broker-sold vehicles, from which, in retrospect, they should have stayed far away. Other common broker-related regrets were buying through friends and selling otherwise good investments solely on a broker's advice.

Selling an investment just because it was down.   Looking to bail when the going gets tough is a natural human tendency. This mistake reminds me of the time my family was headed to a summer beach vacation. Along the way, we drove by an old van along the highway. Outside of the van, about half a dozen members of a band stood and watched as their vehicle went up in flames. Clearly, these folks responded intelligently to the early signs of danger and got out while they still could. Thus, it makes sense that when an investment goes down in value, we want to hit the eject button before our money completely vanishes before our eyes. However, even the best investments have their down periods, and your short-term pessimism could cause you to sell right before prices surge. History has proven again and again that investors who dump stocks, in general, after major stock market declines miss out on enormous future gains.

Putting off investment decisions.   Although I am an advocate of taking your time when investing significant sums of money, a fair number of folks who need decent returns to accomplish their goals sit on cash for years due to fear of losing money, lack of education, and not researching good investments. Take, for example, one successful executive who confided to me that he kept all of his spare funds in low-interest bank accounts because his father had lost everything during the great stock market crash of 1929.

Purchasing or selling investments impulsively.   Wanting to get the next item off their to-do lists, some type-A personalities too quickly toss their money into inappropriate or poorly re-searched investments. I see this happen quite often with people picking individual stocks, rolling over retirement money, and choosing a new investment to replace maturing certificates of deposit (CDs).

Taking investment advice from poor sources.   Friends and rela-tives top the suppliers-of-bad-investing-ideas list, followed closely by the news media and columnists. Too often, insecure people rationalize acting on others' picks by thinking that others are far more in the know.

Selling a home soon after its purchase.   Buying and then selling property entails relatively enormous transaction costs. Impatient and time-pressed buyers sometimes just want to "get it over with" and "get back to their lives." These buyers often make poor purchase decisions and soon find out that they either have to sell the house due to financial considerations or want to sell it based on other factors that could've been more thoroughly researched.

Investing in real estate without understanding cash-flow considerations.   The wealth-building potential of rental-property ownership seems to be on just about everyone's mind these days. Novice real estate investors often make the mistake of not thoroughly researching the income and expense realities of properties before they buy them. Inexperienced landlords also make mistakes when trying to rent their properties and end up with more vacancies and headaches than they expected. Thus, the early years of rental-property ownership can be filled with unexpected losses, which, in the worst cases, have bankrupted owners who were already stretched thin because of the initial purchase price.

Failing to buy needed insurance.   Every day, people lacking health insurance go to the hospital, people without disability insurance end up with long-term disabilities, and people lacking life insurance pass away and leave their loved ones financially strapped. In addition to the danger of exposing yourself and dependents to catastrophic losses, if you fail to get necessary insurance and you develop a medical problem (known to insurers as a preexisting condition), you may be prevented from getting future coverage.

Getting duped into buying the wrong kind (cash value) of life insurance.   Over the years, many clients complained about misleading sales pitches and projections from life insurance brokers. In the worst cases, people funneled money into costly and low-return cash-value plans that offered no up-front tax breaks instead of taking advantage of excellent retirement savings options through employers or plans for the self-employed.

Even Bigger Regrets

In getting to know my clients, I discovered an even bigger set of mistakes that many of them made and sometimes noted. Although some of these errors have a financial loss associated with them, most of them proved to be far costlier in personal ways.

Although I see virtue in having a good work ethic, some "successful" workers go too far. They sacrifice their relationships with family and friends and their personal health for the sake of their careers. Life is short, and too much of it can be spent focusing on material definitions of success—getting ahead at work and making more money, beginning yet another round of home improvements, or shopping away the weekends. Think about your best times with family and friends, and you surely recognize how important your personal connections are. Nurture and cultivate these relationships or they will wither from neglect.

Neglect your marriage enough (or have an affair) and you'll experience some very tangible personal and financial losses when you end up like so many other Americans who are divorced. I'll be the first to agree that some marriages are best off ended through divorce. However, I will also tell you that divorced men and women often end up miserable in subsequent marriages. Divorce typically wreaks havoc on kids and can be financially devastating.

Examining Your Money Mind-Set

In order to identify, accept, and overcome the money-related obstacles that are currently preventing you from reaching a place in life where you're satisfied with what you have—financially *and* personally—you need to start by getting a handle on what I'll call your "money history," particularly the influence of your parents, your childhood, young adult environments, and medical problems.

Before she visited my office seeking financial advice, Eva had made repeated attempts at various times in her twenties and thirties to learn how to invest her retirement savings, which she kept in a low-interest bank account. She subscribed to *Money* magazine, read the business section of her city's newspaper, enrolled in an adult education course at a local college, and discussed investments with coworkers and friends. However, every information-gathering initiative ended with the same result: Eva couldn't bring herself to move her money from her bank account into riskier and higher-potential-return investments like stocks and bonds. Eva, a bright professional woman, wasn't able to realize the impact that her upbringing had on her adult views of the investing world until she was in her forties.

In recalling an incident that occurred at the tender age of seven, Eva finally got to the bottom of her anxieties concerning investments.

> My mom was always complaining about how my father lost money gambling in the stock market. My father was working with this broker who encouraged lots of trading. When the broker switched to a new firm, he mailed out an announcement letter to our home. After my mother opened it in front of me, she tore it

into many pieces and vowed that my father wasn't going to squander any more of our needed money. We were always scraping by for money, so my mother got very angry at my father's investment losses.

This wasn't an isolated scene. Eva realized that, as a child and young adult, she constantly received negative messages at home about investing.

Though the impact of such family tension may be obvious to outside observers, for Eva it didn't become clear until she met with me and discussed her financial history. Eva benefited from learning that stocks and investing weren't gambling or that complicated. She came to understand that her father's broker was encouraging her father's excessive trading, which was detrimental to her dad's investing success.

Eva's story illustrates how one's family history can influence current views on personal finance. However, it's only one example. Other experiences can be even more difficult to interpret, even for outside observers. Taking a historical inventory isn't easy, but if you put in the time and want to challenge yourself and your beliefs, the process can be productive. Eva's story also illustrates the second part of analyzing your money mind-set—examining your current views and behaviors.

Set aside time—about an hour should do—for some personal reflection, ideally in a place where and at a time when you'll be free from distractions. Go to the library, the beach, a coffee shop, or some other place that, ideally, is away from your home. Get out some paper, and answer the following questions:

1. What personal experiences (good and bad) relating to money do you recall from your childhood?

Did you work as a kid and teenager? What lessons did you take away from these experiences? If you didn't work, think about why you didn't and what your parents said to you about working and making money.

2. What memories of your parents (or other guardians) do you have that relate to finances?

Were your parents spenders or savers? What financial crises occurred, and how did your parents handle them? Did money cause tension and problems at home? If you don't have many explicit recollections about money with your caregivers, what implicit messages did you take away from how they led their lives and the role that money played?

3. What efforts did your mom and dad make to teach you about money?

How much freedom and latitude did they give you with money? What lessons did you take away from this? If you had to summarize their philosophy and approach to money in a sentence or two, what would it be?

4. How important were financial considerations in what you chose to study and what jobs and career you sought out?

Did you pursue work based upon what interested you or what you believed you could make more money at? Were you pushed into your career by someone else for the supposed financial security you could achieve?

5. Thinking back to your childhood and young adult years, what significant events happened to you and your family that impacted how you felt about money?

These events could include, for example, a major illness, a parent being laid off, volunteer work you did, and the like. You need not have a long laundry list of major events—the two or three most important and formative occurrences will do.

Having taken the time to reflect upon your background and how it colors how you relate to money, take the next step and spend some time consciously reflecting on your current feelings and attitudes toward money. Can you identify with any of the following?

1. Are you stressed about money?
2. Are you frequently juggling bills and trying to figure out whom to pay next?
3. Do you watch your investments daily or not look at your investment statements out of fear?
4. Are you looking for a hot investment tip that could multiply your money quickly?
5. What financial secrets are you keeping from your spouse (and others)? What would cause you feelings of humiliation and embarrassment?

Remember that there are no right or wrong answers to these questions. In working with clients, I've found that simply taking the time to think about and reflect upon one's history with money provides invaluable insights that enable one to cultivate better financial habits. Quite often, people who go through this process say things like, "I never took the time to consider why I do what I do with money or even what I'm doing." Don't beat yourself up if you can't handle developing thoughtful responses all in one sitting. Some people find these questions bring up strong memories and emotions, so you may need two or three sessions to complete this task.

Common Money Hang-Ups

When we think of a person's personality, adjectives such as *outgoing, temperamental,* and *fun loving* come to mind, but we all have a "money personality" as well. As with our overall personality, we all have some strengths and weaknesses when it comes to our financial disposition. I've structured much of the rest of this book around addressing the weaknesses that we all have. Here are the major areas that I cover:

Excessive spenders and debtors.   We are a consumer nation, and discretionary spending is needed to keep our economy on track. However, far too many people invest far too much of their time and money in shopping for and acquiring the latest consumer items. Without a doubt, the number-one personal financial problem I've seen over the years is excessive spending and accumulation of high-cost consumer debt.

Workaholics.   A consultant whom I used to work for once said to me that she finally became happy with her life after she realized that instead of fitting her life around work, she should endeavor to fit work into the rest of her life. Spurred by personal-consumption desires and the corporate cultures of many businesses, workaholism is a major problem in the United States.

Herd followers and information junkies.   Many people's emotions (greed and fear often being the stars of the show) get the better of them when it comes to investing. The unfortunate result is that people pile into overheated investments, dump those that are depressed and currently out of fashion, and succumb far too frequently to impulsive trades caused by what I call the noise (news) of the day.

Obsessive behaviors.   Gambling and other addictions almost always entail severe financial consequences. Conquering such problems is hard work, first to overcome the denial that typically accompanies addictions and then to get proper treatment.

Extreme savers.   Though they occupy a minority position in the grand scheme of mistaken money mind-sets, a surprising number of people save too much money and have related problems with hoarding and cheating. Oversavers often have related issues to deal with, such as workaholism and fear of losing money when investing.

Avoiders.   Some folks chronically put off dealing with their finances. I've found that these people are often disorganized as well. Although I can't promise you that you'll ever view money management as one of your favorite activities, I can assure you that with the right approach, you can gain control over your financial affairs and have them become positive rather than negative parts of your life.

Conflicting couples.   Love and money often don't mix, and nearly every couple has problems dealing with money. Each of us brings our unique money personality to relationships, and disagreements and conflicts are inevitable. You can learn to recognize your differences and how to best compromise.

Financially challenged children.   Kids aren't born knowing how to properly spend, save, and invest money, so they'll learn. In the absence of your good guidance, children often learn bad habits from our culture—living now, overspending, racking up consumer debt, and so on. You must take steps to teach your kids sound financial habits.

Although you can jump to the specific chapters that you think will most immediately benefit you, I encourage you to read the entire book. Even though, for example, you may feel that you have no issues with gambling or other addictive behaviors, you will benefit from reading that material to gain further insight into what you do well versus what you don't do so well in handling your finances.

My goal is to change the way you think about and relate to money for the better. I want you to get much more from the money that passes through your hands. I'd like you to enjoy your life more, be less stressed about work, and broaden your narrow focus on making more money. One of my goals is to help you recognize and conquer (or at least control) the cultural issues that lead you to focus so much on consumption and following investments too closely.

THE SHOPPER: SHOPPING, SPENDING, AND DEBT ACCUMULATION

Around the time I turned forty, I became motivated to learn more about personal health and nutrition issues. With the demands of work and family, I wasn't exercising as much as I used to, I started gaining a modest amount of weight, and I just didn't feel as energetic and healthy as I did in my twenties and early thirties. In the process of becoming more aware of all things healthy, one habit that I soon changed was not reading food nutrition labels.

As my personal health project got under way, I noticed that one of the grocery stores where my family shopped didn't put nutrition labels on their extensive line of in-house prepared foods. I called and spoke with their "kitchen director" who told me that these helpful labels weren't required by law. Plus, she went on to say, developing these labels and placing them on every product would be very time consuming. She then asked me how such labels might influence my purchasing decisions. Five minutes further into our conversation, this same employee made a confession: they'd applied nutrition labels to their bakery products six years earlier—and sales plummeted. Some customers even complained that they didn't like the labels because they didn't want to know what they were eating! I was shocked, until it dawned on me that I used to be a consumer who never read and couldn't make sense of nutrition labels.

Having worked for many years as a financial counselor, teacher, and columnist fielding questions from readers, I can tell you that, without a doubt, some of the most difficult financial problems to confront involve spending and borrowing habits. As with your health, though, if you don't face the truth now, you'll face far more severe consequences in the future. An even better reason, though, to change your spending views and habits now is the peace of mind and serenity that comes with being more in control and on the path to financial fitness.

At a corporate retirement savings plan presentation I once attended, the investment firm running the 401(k) plan sent in a bunch of guys dressed in fancy three-piece suits. These slick-looking officials conducted a lengthy presentation and droned on about various investments and strategies. The company's benefits manager expressed disappointment to me about how few employees attended these presentations and participated in the retirement savings plan. The reason was pretty clear to me— many people in the company, like most Americans, were living paycheck to paycheck and couldn't participate in the plan until they cut their spending. The investment company presenters were out of touch.

Consumer Debt:
Why People Buy Things They Often Don't Need

The *majority* of Americans carry consumer debt. When I first learned this fact as a young consultant in the early 1980s, I was astonished. And to this day it continues to amaze me that about two-thirds of all American households currently carry credit card and other consumer debt on a month-to-month basis. If you have credit card debt or auto loans, take some solace in the fact that you're far from alone and that many others have overcome these hurdles. But, just as many Americans don't get enough exercise or eat a balanced and healthy diet, being in the majority doesn't make these habits healthy. So don't think that consumer debt is a fine thing—because it's not.

I've long called consumer debt "bad debt" because it carries relatively high interest rates and you get no tax breaks on the interest paid. Examples of consumer debt include auto loans, credit card debt, and finance-company loans. Easy access to consumer debt is one of the leading reasons that consumers overspend, buy things that they don't need, and spend money that they don't have. Consumer debt is the financial equivalent of cancer. Once it starts growing, it can easily get out of control as the high interest charges pile up on top of the debt. And, of course, there's the temptation to keep spending and taking on even more debt.

Calculating the Costs

Overspending leads to a plethora of long-term personal and financial consequences—feeling trapped in unfulfilling work, delayed retirement, divorce, and increased taxes. (Many consumer purchases are taxed at the state or local level or both, and the more you spend, the less able you are to fund retirement accounts and gain the accompanying tax breaks.) Before you know it, you can end up in over your head, spiraling toward bankruptcy. You may think that bankruptcy can't happen to you and that you can handle servicing your debt (for example, by meeting the minimum payment requirements every month). However, an unexpectedly long period of unemployment, a major family medical issue, or some other unanticipated problem can tilt the balance and make the debt unmanageable. And with some consumer debt, such as credit card debt, it may take you decades to pay it off if you simply make the minimum payment!

Other costs of consumer debt are the lost investing opportunities you could be taking advantage of with the money currently going to service the debt and accumulating interest. Though having thousands or even tens of thousands in consumer debt is ugly enough, even uglier is the fact that decades from now, money invested rather than spent on this debt could have mushroomed into hundreds of thousands of dollars.

Since 1980, the number of personal bankruptcies has more than tripled. During the economic boom of the 1990s, more than 1 in 10 households filed personal bankruptcy. By comparison, during the Great Depression of the 1930s, just 1 out of every 215 filed bankruptcy. (While changes to the personal-bankruptcy laws in 2005 made it harder to file, we still see plenty of filings.)

Reviewing Your Views on Debt

Although some Americans are in hock due to devastating events beyond their control, such as large medical expenses or job losses, the vast majority of people with consumer debt end up in that position because their spending exceeds their income, and consumer borrowings close that gap. The baby boomer generation was really the first to use and abuse consumer debt. Jay Westbrook, a law professor, conducted an extensive study of people who filed personal bankruptcy and found that the typical filers were well-educated, middle-class baby boomers who overconsumed with credit cards.

The simple truth is that credit cards and other consumer debt enable you to spend money that you don't have. We Americans have a warped sense of what we "need" because so many of us base our expectations on what we see and hear around us. Our peers drive newer, costlier cars, so we think and believe that we "need" one (or two or three) of those as well. We convince ourselves that in order for our children to become well educated and happy, they "need" to be raised in a luxurious home in a town that supposedly has the best schools. We think that to be viewed as successful, attractive, and with it, we "need" to buy the things that advertisers endlessly bombard us with.

Whether the products are option-packed cars, high-end home appliances, or the latest designer clothing, marketers motivate consumers to buy on emotion rather than need. Marketers also play on insecurities, fears, and guilt and suggest that you can feel better about yourself and loved ones by buying their products. You won't be able to overcome this common and constant problem of overspending and wracking up consumer debt until you recognize these pressures and how they poison your worldview and buying decisions.

An eye-opening and at times disturbing book to read is Pamela Danzinger's *Why People Buy Things That They Don't Need* (Paramount Market Publishing). Danzinger runs a consulting firm that advises large consumer-product companies on how to design products and convince consumers to buy them. She correctly points out that much of American consumer purchases are discretionary: "The simple fact is that the contemporary American lives so far above subsistence, we have lost touch with the basic needs of life: food for nutrition, basic clothing, and shelter for warmth and protection."

The central thesis of Danzinger's book is that consumer-product companies can induce people to buy costly products they don't really need by appealing to the consumer's desires and emotional needs. As she goes on to state, "In today's consumer driven society, satisfying consumer needs has less to do with the practical meeting of physical needs and everything to do with gratifying desires based upon emotions. The act of consuming, rather than the item being consumed, satisfies the need."

I know that for people who came of age during my grandparents' and parents' generations, during and after the Great Depression, for example, such consumption indulgences weren't the norm. My middle-class parents never borrowed to buy anything except the modest home my brother, sister, and I were raised in. Think about that. It has really been in the past couple of generations that we, as a society, have grown quite accustomed to buying consumer items on credit. "Spoiled the younger generations may be, but they are the consumers who express their wants, desires, and dreams in terms of needs and necessities because they have never done without," writes Danzinger. "Need can wait, but want and desire drive purchases." Danzinger and her consulting firm identify fourteen so-called justifiers (I'd probably call them rationalizations) that consumers employ when making discretionary purchases. Improving the quality of your life; buying on impulse; replacing an existing item (for instance, an older sofa), which leads to purchasing numerous related items (armchairs and end tables); and purchasing certain goods for status are examples of common justifiers. The goal of consumer-product companies and their marketing staff is to persuade and cajole you into buying what they're selling even if you don't really need it. Remember this the next time the thought goes through your mind that you want or need to buy something that isn't a necessity.

This appeal to emotional fulfillment rather than need fulfillment isn't limited to the marketing of products. Personal services are increasingly being sold on this basis as well. Witness the number of television shows that do extreme makeovers on people's bodies. A cosmetic surgeon in *Forbes* was quoted as saying, "If someone comes in to see you and you are fat and a little sloppy, right away you put them off, and you're probably not going to get a second chance. People think that this person does not take care of himself, so he won't be conscientious in the workplace."

Dr. Phil McGraw had an interesting show about the public's obsessions and addictions with movie stars—trying to dress like them, buying things that they have, and even having plastic surgery to try to look like them. There was extensive discussion about the celebrity magazines and how reading those publications and watching television shows like *Entertainment Tonight* feed such addictions. To change this mind-set, you first must recognize the source of the problem and then take action to do something positive to address it. Stopping the magazine subscriptions and not watching the particular television programs are major steps in the right direction. Individual counseling may help identify emotional voids.

The Truth about the Credit Card Business

One of my first assignments as a management consultant in the financial services industry in the early 1980s was to conduct a product-line profitability study for a regional bank. Consultants got paid a lot of money to do this type of analysis, which basi-cally helped a company figure out how much (or little) profit it made on various products and services. It was no great surprise to our team that the bank's credit card business was much more profitable than its other lines of business. We found that banks, in general, routinely had a profit margin that was five to six times higher, despite charge-offs (loan losses), from credit cards compared with their other lines of business.

Banks committed to the credit card business are quite sophis-ticated in identifying consumers likely to borrow a lot on their credit cards and thus be profitable to the bank. For example, Shailesh Mehta, the longtime chief executive officer (CEO) of Providian Financial, a major player in the credit card business, routinely pockets more than $10 million annually in compensa-tion. How does one get to such a lofty position and garner such incredible paydays? In part, by making credit cards as profitable as they now are for one's employer. Mehta, a "mathematical ge-nius," developed the computer models used by Providian to identify middle- and lower-income consumers likely to borrow a lot. He was hailed by a former MasterCard president as one of the brightest and most able people in the business. In a *New York Times* article about his bank's credit card strategies, Mehta said, "Credit is very important to people; it is the ability to acquire things. We want to grant people the maximum possible credit line, and we get compensated for taking that risk."

Not surprisingly, lower-income households carry the heaviest burden of credit card debt in relation to their incomes. Among households with annual incomes below $40,000, the average credit card debt carried amounts to more than 10 percent of their household income. Banks target and push high-limit credit cards to these people most likely to get hooked on them.

The banks then add insult to injury by hitting them with poorly disclosed and outrageous interest rates. Major credit card purveyors, which have heavily promoted supposed low-interest-rate cards, really whack you if you make a couple of late payments. A 9 percent interest rate can quickly mushroom to 25 percent or higher! You may also be hit with $35 late fees, which raise your effective interest rate even higher.

Just three weeks before the 2004 presidential election, Federal Reserve chairman Alan Greenspan gave a speech to the American Community Bankers in Washington, D.C., in which he discussed, among other topics, the near record levels of debt carried by American consumers. As quoted by *Bloomberg Business News*, Greenspan said, "Credit card debt has risen in large part because households prefer the convenience of cards as a method of payment, and hence, the increase does not necessarily indicate greater financial stress." Greenspan, who is a political appointee as the Fed chairman, clearly doesn't understand or isn't willing to admit the problem facing so many Americans—a *documented* problem (in such places as the Westbrook study that I mentioned earlier). The fact is that the majority of American households carries a significant amount of debt on cards and are not simply using credit cards as a convenient payment method.

How Auto Buying Has Changed for the Worse

Another venue in which using consumer debt is now totally accepted as normal and commonplace is the car lot. Several years ago, I walked into a local auto dealer. I was in the market for a lightly used sedan that had good safety features. I knew the models I was interested in weren't cheap, which was why I sought a preowned vehicle. After speaking with a salesperson and test-driving a car that I liked, the topic of price and financing came up. He pushed hard for me to lease a new car, telling me what a great deal it was. When I told him that I didn't wish to buy a car that way, or even with an auto loan, he said in a somewhat annoyed tone, "What are you, a communist?" Although I couldn't believe how rude he'd been, it was yet more evidence of the pressure that salespeople, in particular, and our consumer society, in general, put on us to do (or should I say buy) what everyone else is supposedly doing (buying).

Auto salespeople are trained to sell new cars through auto loans or leasing by focusing your attention on the monthly payment (for example, $399, $499, and so on) and diverting your attention from the sticker price of the vehicle ($20,000, $25,000, or more) and the total cost, including financing. Auto dealer ads on television and radio barely mention the sticker price anymore, and it's usually buried in the fine print in the newspaper. The monthly leasing or loan payment, however, is *huge* and won't be missed or forgotten.

When I wrote my first book, *Personal Finance for Dummies,* the editors at that book's publishing company (IDG Books) were incredulous that I was advising readers to *not* borrow and *not* take out a lease to buy a car. How, my editors, asked, did I expect people to buy expensive new cars with cash only? I said that if someone doesn't have enough saved to buy a new car without a hefty loan or a lease, then they shouldn't be buying such an expensive car—or a *new* car—in the first place! We spoiled Americans don't stop to consider that most people around the globe don't own a car, let alone a brand-spanking-new one fresh off the assembly line. What about buying a good-quality used auto?

You can give yourself a world of perspective without driving far from home: Go visit a soup kitchen, shelter for the homeless, or another place frequented by the poor. Spend some time in a small town or section of a city where middle-class and poor people live. You won't see many new, expensive cars during these visits. Now, I do sometimes get questions from readers implying that I'm out of touch with car-buying realities because I'm a "rich and successful" author and businessman. Although I am more economically secure than I was many years ago, my car-buying views and practices haven't changed. Although I can and do buy costlier cars than I did when I was fresh out of college more than twenty years ago, I live within my means and still buy only what I can afford to purchase without borrowing or leasing.

The average cost of a new car today is closing in on $30,000! Over the years, auto prices have risen faster than incomes, so automakers and dealers have developed plenty of ways to keep monthly loan or lease payments reasonable enough to entice consumers to buy such costly cars. Loan terms have been stretched from three years to five years, and now to as many as seven or eight years. But there's an additional upside to stretching out loan terms so people can "afford" costlier cars. Auto manufacturers have been happily pushing longer-term loans to develop another route to your pocketbook—by enriching their financing subsidiaries that originate most auto loans. Those increasingly common no- or low-money-down deals aren't public-service campaigns.

And neither are the low- or no-interest-rate loans that manufacturers and dealers provide to get you behind the wheel of a new car that's over your head financially. Those terms are nothing more than gimmicks that lack the following important

disclosure: "If you take this loan at the ridiculously low advertised interest rate, you might as well forget getting a competitive
price on the car because we will have to soak you." Don't be
fooled by the low advertised interest rates: the two largest U.S.
automakers (General Motors and Ford) now make more money
from their financing divisions than they do from selling cars!
Rather than thinking of those companies as automakers, investment analysts think of them as banks that happen to sell cars as
an inducement to get people to take out loans.

Not only does financing auto purchases lead people to buy
more expensive cars than they can truly afford, but increasing
numbers of American families are also buying second, third,
and even fourth cars they don't truly need and can't afford.

The Faces (and Lessons) of Bankruptcy

All of the temptations, expectations, and pressures too often
add up to big consumer-debt problems, which eventually tip
people over the brink financially. This section highlights some
real-life cases that ended up in bankruptcy and shows the kinds
of people that this can happen to, how they ended up in trouble, and, most important, what the consequences were, especially the nonfinancial results.

Sara grew up in a family where she and the other children got
fabulous presents at the holidays even though her family was
poor. "I picked up my parents' habit of living in the moment
and spending money as soon as you earn it," she says. Sara is a
self-employed consultant with a master's degree from an Ivy
League university. She asked that her real name not be used because she's ashamed of her financial habits and worried about
how her colleagues at work will view her. However, like many

people in her situation, Sara doesn't know how common over-spending and debt accumulation are among her peers.

In her sixth year of marriage, Sara left her job at a large corporation to start her own company. She was doing what she loved, and everything seemed to be going right. In the early months of her business, she earned little income. Sara carried credit card debt before starting her business. However, her outstanding balances grew as she developed her business and continued spending money as before when she was working for an employer at a generous salary with benefits.

Meanwhile, Sara's husband was growing increasingly upset with her spending. He was a saver and disliked her carrying credit card balances at double-digit interest rates. Sometimes he paid Sara's outstanding debt, just to relieve his own anxieties. Upon starting her own business, Sara used the increased flexibility in her schedule to indulge in one of her passions—dance. But her husband grew resentful of the time she spent with the dance troupe given her spending, debt, and low business income. He worked hard at his job and believed that he was carrying far too much of the household's financial burden.

Rather than scaling back on her purchases to compensate for her reduced income, Sara's wallet full of plastic tempted her like a stocked liquor cabinet tempts an alcoholic. She was addicted to her multiple credit lines, which gave her the ability to live a lifestyle beyond her means. But much like alcoholism, Sara says that her addiction was ultimately unsustainable and contributed heavily to the failure of her marriage. After her divorce, with her husband's income and belongings gone, Sara's spending actually increased because she had to repurchase items that she and her husband had jointly owned, such as a car, which she bought on credit. Meanwhile, "My mailbox was brimming with credit card offers," says Sara, adding, "The pleasure from spending became more enticing given the personal loss I suffered." Sara's debt mushroomed.

Within four years, Sara was drowning in more than $30,000 of credit card and credit-line debts. She was often short on cash, so she began charging necessities such as groceries and using credit card cash-advance checks to pay her rent. Meanwhile, the initial "teaser" interest rates on her credit cards went from 9 and 10 percent to 15 and 18 percent. With an annual income of just $35,000, Sara could barely keep up with the mounting interest payments. Paying down the debt balance seemed impossible.

Her savior appeared to come in an unexpected six-figure consulting contract that provided hope for finally ridding herself of the high-interest consumer debt. However, fulfilling the contract was more expensive than she had expected due to high costs in hiring subcontractors. Stressed, exhausted, and unable to come up with her required quarterly income-tax payments on her business income, Sara filed personal bankruptcy. Following on the heels of the failure of her marriage, Sara was now bankrupt financially as well as emotionally.

Duane Garrett hosted a radio show I sometimes listened to. He was a popular talk-show host and attorney, the campaign chairman for Diane Feinstein's senatorial races, and friend of Vice President Al Gore. Garrett introduced Ted Kennedy at a Democratic National Convention and was the president of a sports-memorabilia auction house he owned with two other partners. He was married with two daughters and owned a hilltop home in much-sought-after Tiburon, in Marin County, near San Francisco. As the *San Francisco Chronicle* said, "Garrett appeared to have everything in life—fame, money, family."

One day, when I happened to be listening to his program, I was struck by Garrett lamenting that he was having trouble losing weight and needed solutions. I called his show for the first time, got on the air, and offered him some words of encouragement. I told him that it seemed to me that he needed to exercise regularly. He quickly cut me off, his voice sounding almost panicked, saying that he didn't have time to mess around with exercise. I tried relaying my experiences—that I found myself far more productive at work and other endeavors when I was refreshed from exercise—but it was clear he wasn't interested.

A few weeks later, I heard on the local news that Garrett's body had been found floating near the Golden Gate Bridge. Garrett, the family man, successful entrepreneur, and mingler with political heavyweights, had chosen to end his own life by leaping to his death from the bridge. In the subsequent weeks and months, it came out that his business was in trouble. He had accumulated more than $11 million in debt, including having heavily mortgaged his home, and had just $600,000 in assets. He'd been borrowing extensively from friends and business associates to pay off debts. "Ultimately the scheme became so frenetic that Garrett took his own life rather than go through what he perceived as the humiliation of bankruptcy," reported the *San Francisco Chronicle* after interviewing Garrett's friends. Interestingly, that same paper had written an article in the aftermath of his suicide in which it stated that Garrett "was so entangled in a web of debt and deceit that he routinely bilked investors who were his friends and associates." It further referred to his borrowing from Peter to pay Paul as a "Ponzi-type scheme." So, even in death, Garrett was humiliated, perhaps unfairly. From what I read of Garrett's dealings, his business nose-dived partly due to his mismanagement and misjudgments (hey, none of us is perfect) but also due to the sports-memorabilia market souring for a time, which, of course, was totally beyond his control.

Like so many baby boomers, Garrett chased after the "good life." He bought an expensive home in an exclusive neighborhood, owned a large fishing boat, collected costly art, and drove luxury automobiles. His business failed. Failure is part of the small-business world. Because he was so burdened with debt, it became clear to him that he couldn't dig himself out of the situation. The shame of his personal financial condition, debts, and failure is what led Garrett to kill himself.

COUPLES' SECRETS

Married Americans were surveyed by the research firm Ipsos-NPD to learn what secrets they keep from their spouses. On the list were the usual suspects, such as extramarital affairs and attractions to other people. Failures at work and personal dreams and aspirations were other commonly concealed topics. The number-one issue married couples covered up, though, was how much they spend. One woman told the market-research firm conducting the survey, "I don't like to tell him how much I spend when I go shopping. I'm afraid he'll cut back on the budget." But this pattern of secrecy didn't rest solely with wives—husbands hid details of their purchases from their wives about as often as the women duped the men in their lives.

Compulsive Spenders and Debtors

A wealth of recent research now shows that some people are compulsive spenders and shoppers. This concept is no great surprise to observers of human behavior, including psychologists, therapists, and financial counselors like me who've worked with people with spending problems. Academic researchers and mental health experts agree that for some people, spending money does for them what abusing food, drugs, or alcohol does for others. Compulsive spenders who invest a damaging amount of time and financial resources in shopping typically suffer from anxiety disorders, depression, and low self-esteem. Compulsive shoppers get a "high" from shopping and spending. These feelings of euphoria provide a distraction from and help bury (at least while they're shopping) negative feelings about themselves and their lives.

Compulsive shoppers tend to be female due in part to the fact that women do more of the shopping in households. Gender-related estimates state that as many as nine people in ten with this problem are women. Compulsive shoppers are typically lonely and bored and schedule their lives around shopping. When addicted shoppers hit the stores, they can't leave without making a purchase. They generally buy multiple items financed with credit cards and, in some cases, through repeated home-equity loans.

Do You Have a Shopping Problem?

Debtors Anonymous, an organization patterned after Alcoholics Anonymous, was formed in the mid-1970s by individuals who recognized that some consumers literally could not control their shopping, spending, and debt accumulation habits. This organization has developed a series of questions to help identify

IF ONLY I HAD A FEW MORE MILLION: CELEBRITY SPENDAHOLICS

Many celebrities with millions pouring in end up in financial trouble because they spend it as fast—or faster—than they earn it. Patricia Cornwell, the successful author, was not accustomed to having so much money flowing her way and, by her own admission, went on "impulsive shopping sprees." In addition to fighting spending problems, Cornwell also ended up in alcohol rehab after smashing her car. Mike Tyson, the former heavyweight boxing champion, filed bankruptcy despite having earned more than $300 million during his career. Hard as it is to believe, Tyson's out-of-control spending on mansions, cars, jewelry, exotic animals, and extravagant gifts consumed his gargantuan paydays. And the Michael Jackson trial highlighted the fact that the famous pop singer has had similar spending problems.

Celebrity spendaholics underscore the important lesson that it's not what you make but what you're able to save and keep. Earning more money won't necessarily solve your money woes. Learning to live within your means and conquering problems relating to excess spending will help you accomplish your financial and personal goals.

whether a person is a compulsive spender. They say that most compulsive debtors will answer yes to at least eight of the following fifteen questions:

1. Are your debts making your home life unhappy?
2. Does the pressure of your debts distract you from your daily work?

3. Are your debts affecting your reputation?

4. Do your debts cause you to think less of yourself?

5. Have you ever given false information in order to obtain credit?

6. Have you ever made unrealistic promises to your creditors?

7. Does the pressure of your debts make you careless of the welfare of your family?

8. Do you ever fear that your employer, family, or friends will learn the extent of your total indebtedness?

9. When faced with a difficult financial situation, does the prospect of borrowing give you an inordinate feeling of relief?

10. Does the pressure of your debts cause you to have difficulty sleeping?

11. Has the pressure of your debts ever caused you to consider getting drunk?

12. Have you ever borrowed money without giving adequate consideration to the rate of interest you are required to pay?

13. Do you usually expect a negative response when you are subject to a credit investigation?

14. Have you ever developed a strict regimen for paying off your debts, only to break it under pressure?

15. Do you justify your debts by telling yourself that you are superior to the "other" people, and when you get your "break" you'll be out of debt overnight?

Compulsive spending can be a devastating behavior, but a misaligned mind-set toward spending and shopping that doesn't reach that level can also severely affect your financial and personal well-being. Although there's no perfect diagnostic test to see whether you or someone you care about has a problem with shopping and spending, the following questions are a good starting point.

- Do you feel guilty about shopping?
- Do you argue with your spouse or partner about shopping? Do you hide purchases or receipts or lie about what you've bought?
- Does shopping reduce the time you spend with your kids, friends, or family? Do you use shopping as an escape from difficulties and unhappiness at home?
- Is your shopping causing financial trouble? (A certain level of affluence can rule out this particular result.)
- Are the shopping, spending, and accumulated debt leading to feelings of helplessness, anger, confusion, fear, or depression?
- Do the act of shopping and the accompanying interaction with salespeople give you a feeling of worth, importance, and control?
- Do you tend to accumulate items, including duplicates and triplicates of items that you never use?
- Are the costs associated with shopping, in terms of time and financial resources, negatively impacting your overall personal health and well-being?

Strategies for Overcoming Overspending

Throughout this chapter, I've discussed common spending problems and how to begin to change the harmful mind-set associated with them. Now it's time to take action to get your spending under control once and for all. From my years of working as a financial counselor, I've come to realize that telling people to reduce their spending is like telling an overweight person to just lose weight. Easier said than done. The fundamental problem is that following a budget or a diet is simply unpleasant and often doesn't attack the root causes of the problem (what you choose to read, watch, and emulate). That's why I don't think diets or budgets are the solution for most people. This budget focus is why many credit counseling services fail to help solve debt-related problems.

Most people are relieved to hear me say that I don't think instituting dollar-by-dollar budgets is the solution. You don't need to track where and when you spend every dollar. What you should do, however, is get out your checkbook register, credit card statements, and anything else that will help you detail where you spend your money in a typical month. And don't overlook your cash purchases, such as those daily three-dollar lattes and ten-dollar lunches. Track these cash purchases for a week or two in a small notebook that you carry with you. Determining where your money has been going should help you to identify some fat to cut. This approach works because you're not planning all of your spending in advance—which is a nearly impossible and utterly joyless task. What you are doing is examining your general spending and making focused and targeted cuts.

If overspending continues to plague you after you've trimmed the fat from your spending and instituted the changes I recommend in the following sections, contact a local chapter of Debtors Anonymous (check your local phone directory) or visit their Web site at http://www.debtorsanonymous.org.

Curtail Your Credit Cards

The biggest problem with overspending is consumer debt and its availability. So, if you tend to spend too much using credit cards and consumer loans, you have to remove the root of the problem. Cut up and rid yourself of your credit cards. Believe it or not, you don't "need" a credit card to function in modern society. Cash and checks worked just fine before credit cards were commonplace, and they still do. Get yourself a VISA or MasterCard *debit card*. These cards are connected to your checking account or money-market fund and thus prevent you from spending money that you don't have. Check with your current bank and others in the area. Plus, increasing numbers of the larger mutual fund companies such as Fidelity, T. Rowe Price, and Vanguard are offering asset-management accounts that come with unlimited check writing and debit cards, although more of these accounts are available for higher-balance customers.

If you want to keep one credit card for, say, an occasional car rental, how about putting it in a water-filled container in your freezer and thawing it out only for one-time usage? The approach may seem a bit extreme, but the simple fact that you have to make an effort to thaw out the plastic will introduce an added barrier to spur-of-the-moment spending decisions. The time that it takes for you to access the card provides additional time to reconsider. However, don't keep any credit cards that are specific to one merchant (such as department stores). These cards are completely unnecessary, typically have the highest interest rates, and will tempt overspending.

Cutting off the potential source for overspending is the key to forcing yourself to change your spending habits. This transition will be far less painful and far more productive if you first, or simultaneously, implement the other strategies recommended here.

Change the Way You Approach Purchases

To change your consumption habits, you must first change your mind-set about shopping. Typically, this involves changing shopping from a source of entertainment, a distraction from other problems, or an impulse decision to a simple means to an end: acquiring a product that you feel you need and want. Furthermore, you must clearly delineate between necessities and luxuries. Yes, you need transportation, but buying a brand-new $40,000 car isn't necessary. Ditto for your need for a quick escape from the rigors of work and the $7,000 Caribbean vacation.

To get a better handle on how you make consumption decisions, spend some time thinking about how shopping makes you feel. As I discussed earlier in this chapter in the section entitled "Do You Have a Shopping Problem?" some overspenders shop to fill voids in their lives. Answer the questions in that section. Sitting down with a psychologist or other counselor may be beneficial.

Observe friends and relatives who are thrifty and try learning some of their better spending habits. Don't shop with people who share your spending problems or who've often accompanied you on shopping sprees in the past.

Prior to going shopping for necessities that aren't everyday purchases (whether you're physically going shopping, sitting down with catalogs, or connecting to the huge marketplace known as the Internet), make a list of the items you're looking for and do some research first (*Consumer Reports* is a good starting point). After you're sure that you want an item; your research has helped you identify brands, models, and so on that are good values; and you've assessed your bank account to ensure that you can afford it, check various retailers and compare prices. When you set out to make a purchase, only buy what's on your list. The Internet can be a time-efficient tool for performing research and price comparisons, but be careful of two common online problems. The first is advertising that masquerades as informative articles. The second problem is retailers that may be here today and gone tomorrow or who may be unresponsive after the purchase. Of course, this latter problem occurs with traditional bricks-and-mortar retailers, too.

Eliminate Temptation

If you're tempted to buy something you hadn't planned on once you're in a store, make a note of the item and the store's price—and then go home without it! Do some thinking and research the product, returning to the steps I suggest above. If you're sure you still want the item, and you can afford it, then start shopping on the basis of price.

Eliminate temptations to shop and spend more. Toss out mail-order catalogs that clutter your mailbox, and don't click on ads or browse for products online. *Never* watch shopping channels or infomercials on television. Visit the Web site http://www.dmaconsumers.org/consumerassistance.html, and follow the directions for getting off mailing and telemarketing lists. Also visit the Web site http://www.donotcall.gov to enroll in the National Do Not Call Registry. Finally, to reduce the mailings you receive caused by credit bureau information on file about your household, call 1-888-5OPTOUT.

Focus on Value

Always look for the best values for all the products that you buy. By *value,* I mean the level of quality given the price you'd pay for the item. Don't assume that a more expensive product is better, because you often don't get what you pay for. That said, you can sometimes get a significantly better-quality product by paying a modest amount more.

Don't waste money on brand names. If you're like most folks, you've bought products for the status you thought they conveyed or because you simply assumed that a given brand-name product was superior to the alternative choices—without properly researching the issue before making the purchase. But thanks to advertising costs, brand-name products are frequently more expensive than comparable quality but less-well-known brands.

Get your money back when products and services aren't up to snuff or when you realize you really don't need something you recently bought. The process of returning items will get you to think harder before making future purchases and pay some financial dividends.

Consider Saving

Don't begin a saving program until you've paid off your consumer debt. You're very unlikely to earn an investment return, after taxes, that exceeds the relatively high interest costs on credit cards and other common consumer debt.

When you can afford to set some money aside in savings, make your saving automatic by setting up a direct-deposit payroll deduction with your employer (or using automatic checking-account transfers to an investment account if you're self-employed). That way, you're free to spend what's left over, and you don't need to drive yourself and other family members crazy tracking every expenditure.

For tax advantages and protection from your own spending temptations, save inside retirement (tax-sheltered) accounts where possible. Employers offering retirement accounts can set you up with automatic payroll deduction. If you're funding your own retirement accounts (such as an individual retirement account [IRA] or Keogh), mutual fund and other investment companies can help you with establishing automatic investment plans as well.

And remember this: the best part of overcoming overspending isn't just the long-term financial benefits; it's the peace of mind and satisfaction that come with it.

THE WORKAHOLIC:
FITTING LIFE INTO
YOUR WORK

The United States prides itself on its strong work ethic. Our popular history is rooted in ideas of economic self-reliance and the ability of every man (and woman) to pull himself (or herself) up by the bootstraps to carve out a better life. In our culture, burning the midnight oil is worshiped, and the path to success is paved with fifty-, sixty-, and seventy-hour workweeks. And we still love the rags-to-riches stories that give us hope for having a better life. Magazine covers, from *Fortune* and *Forbes* to *People* and *Entertainment Weekly,* along with television shows of all stripes, are filled with the beaming faces of those who came from humble backgrounds to achieve great "success" and wealth. Many of us, of course, feel fortunate to live in a country where we have the freedom and ability to work hard at something of our own choosing to accomplish our goals and dreams.

Consider this career advice from self-made billionaire media mogul Michael Bloomberg in his autobiography, *Bloomberg on Bloomberg:* "The rewards almost always go to those who outwork the others. You've got to come in early, stay late, lunch at your desk, and take projects home nights and weekends." I don't mean to single out Bloomberg (as I'm sure that most presidents and CEOs of large corporations would find little to quibble with in that quote), but I have a hard time identifying with a man who describes his "perfect day" as "one where I'm hopelessly overscheduled . . . to work by 7:00 A.M.; a series of rushed meetings; phone call after phone call; 50 or more voice messages and the same number of e-mails demanding a reply; a hurried business lunch between myriad stand-up conferences to solve firm personnel, financial, and policy problems" that culminates when he "falls into bed, exhausted but satisfied with the day's accomplishments. That's the best weekday one could ever have!"

One magazine appropriately called Bloomberg's autobiography "Confessions of a Workaholic." Though his business acumen is obvious, his lack of success on other fronts, I would argue, is representative of the consequences of leading an unbalanced, workaholic life. Behind nearly every supersuccessful workaholic man (or woman) like Bloomberg lies a personal and family life in tatters—or no family life at all. Bloomberg, I learned, was divorced, childless, and now in his sixties, having spent his adult years mostly married to his work. In my work as a financial counselor, I have observed far too many people—the vast majority of whom have not and will not achieve overwhelming success in their careers—who sacrifice their personal lives, family relationships, and friendships for the sake of working more than is necessary.

Over the years, I've gotten a lot of questions, e-mails, and snail mail about stocks, mutual funds, home buying, and other money topics. Without a doubt, however, I have never received more mail than when I've written about the need to balance work with the rest of one's life and about the decision to take time away from work to raise children. My bias, and I'll be the first to admit that I have one, is that you should spend plenty of time and energy outside of work enjoying your other interests, your friends, and your family. If you have kids, family time is particularly important, and especially when they're young—and I don't define *family time* as you hunched over a pile of work at the table while the kids sit in front of the television. Your kids are young only once, and you don't get any do-overs.

Interestingly, parents say that they do, indeed, want to spend more time with their children. In a survey done for the Boys and Girls Clubs of America and KidsPeace, a whopping 94 percent of parents said that they see a positive relationship between the amount of meaningful time adults spend with children and the manner in which those kids deal with big issues like drugs, alcohol, and discipline. The majority of parents (54 percent), however, said that they had little or no time to spend engaged in activities (physical and educational) with their children. The major impediment that parents cited was their work schedules.

Why Do We Work So Much?

Our culture not only accepts workaholism and the wealth that it sometimes brings but also celebrates it. Not too long ago, I was reading some press clippings that I was sent about a successful computer expert. This tech guru was quoted as saying, "I love what I do; it's the focus of my life right now." Another article described him as "a no-holds-barred, passionate workaholic who often stays in the office until 2 a.m." How sad, I thought, that Mr. Guru was also the father of two young children.

We Are Antifamily: The Role of Corporate Cultures

With increasingly competitive workplace pressures and the higher cost of housing in desired areas, more and more people are working longer hours than they'd like and are best for them. Many employers exacerbate this problem with the culture they foster encouraging and rewarding workaholics.

You've surely heard about the trillions of dollars in lost market value from the bursting of the technology-stock bubble in the early 2000s. If you had money in technology stocks or funds, you've directly experienced that pain. But the biggest and most painful losses from the technology-stock crash weren't financial; they were personal and emotional.

By way of background, a little history is in order here. When stock prices of technology (and especially Internet) companies skyrocketed in the 1990s, venture-capital money flooded toward start-ups. Ground-floor investors and employees sought quick riches from initial public offerings (IPOs). Before the days of the overheated tech market, companies took upwards of ten years to get to the size at which they could go public, but these new start-ups were doing it in a couple of years. These firms were pressure cookers. Workers were seduced by the hope (and, in some cases, greed) that an upcoming IPO would compensate them for eighty-hour workweeks.

Like bartenders and bar owners who profit from big drinkers, corporate (and even nonprofit) managers often implicitly and explicitly support and encourage overworking. Unfortunately, many corporations view extracting more hours from employees as cost-effective—employees on salary are a fixed cost, so the more hours you can squeeze out of your people, theoretically, the more work gets accomplished. Joe Robinson, director of the

Work to Live campaign, comments: "We're the most vacation-starved country in the world. . . . In total hours, we now work two months longer every year than Germans; two weeks longer than the Japanese." But we can't blame workaholism simply on greedy or cheap employers.

Consumption Expectations: Trying to Buy the Good Life

Consumption expectations also play a role in why we work the hours that we do and why career is the focus of so many people's lives. Take the case of Ken, who's trying to live the American dream. Ken attended a top college and then went on to graduate school. Now he's providing for his family, which includes three children. For the past two decades, Ken has logged fifty to sixty-plus hours a week at work climbing to the top tiers of his field. Because of this dogged pursuit of career advancement, he spends little time with his kids but relishes his role as a provider and role model for hard work and responsibility. In addition to working so many hours, another reason that Ken spends so little time with his kids is that they're enrolled in numerous costly after-school activities throughout the week and on the weekends. On the one hand, Ken feels "successful" because he has the means to afford all of these extra programs for his children. On the other hand, he feels an emptiness and lack of connection with his family because they spend so little time together. Despite buying a large home in a premier community with some of the best public schools, Ken's kids have spent many of their school years in the most expensive private schools. And despite having amassed more than $5 million in financial assets, Ken still doesn't feel financially secure enough. He continues to push hard in his career.

Ken's "problem" is extraordinarily typical, especially among men and women who have worked hard for what they have. Early in their careers, folks like Ken generally have little in the way of financial assets and usually have educational debt. In short, they're hungry, willing, and able to put in long and productive hours. Fast-forward ten or twenty years: Debts have shrunk, assets have mushroomed, and people like Ken are well on their way to achieving, or have actually achieved, financial independence. They don't need to continue to work so hard or as many hours (or even at all). When you add the stresses and time demands of raising children to the equation, reassessing your priorities makes even more sense.

My work as a financial counselor and my observations of other parents have demonstrated that the pull and stress of work are especially problematic for families with young children. Parents rationalize their long work hours with a belief that, in the end, time away from their children actually leads to happier kids and better lives. They believe that their incomes enable them to buy a home in a good community, so they're providing a safe environment for their kids and access to better schools. However, educators and child-development experts disagree with parents who believe that aiming for schools in more affluent communities leads to better-educated and happier kids. Kids generally are happier when their parents spend time with them.

Trying to "Have It All" by Overdelegating Parental Tasks

We are increasingly relying on institutions like our schools to raise our children. Over the years, the school day—along with associated after-school activities and after-school child care—has gotten longer. It's not unusual for elementary school–age children to have adult-length days away from home. I'm talking about seven- and eight-year-old children being away from their home from seven in the morning until six or even seven o'clock at night, five days a week! And the fact that this type of schedule is creeping toward the commonplace without more than cursory objections is even scarier. But again, there are rationalizations: increasingly, parents justify high school–like experiences for young children as a means to groom them for admission to the nation's top colleges and universities.

Parenting responsibilities, especially in more affluent communities, are widely viewed as something to be delegated and best avoided. Popular columnists like Anna Quindlen freely disparage motherhood. In a column titled "Playing God on No Sleep: Isn't Motherhood Grand? Do You Want the Real Answer or the Official Hallmark-Card Version?" Quindlen discusses her feelings of disgust upon visiting a doctor's office with her sick child and seeing a cross-stitched sampler on the wall that said, "God could not be everywhere so he made mothers." She wrote this column in part, she said, out of her own "fascination" with the story of Andrea Yates who drowned her five children in a bathtub. Quindlen concludes her piece by reasoning, "If God made mothers because he couldn't be everywhere, maybe he could meet us halfway and eradicate vomiting, and colic too, and the hideous sugarcoating of what we are and what we do that leads to false cheer, easy lies and maybe sometimes something much, much worse, almost unimaginable."

When I first read Quindlen's article, which disgusted me, my twin boys were five years old and my youngest son was two and a half. I was very involved in raising them. I had made a major career change and took a significant pay cut so that I could be home much more. When the twins were infants, I always got up with my wife when they woke up during the night. I changed their diapers and brought them to her for nursing. I then carried them back to their cribs only to repeat the routine two to three hours later. I worked at home most days and helped with meals and taking care of the kids every day. Yes, it was tiring, and yes, I missed out on some work opportunities, but I loved doing it and viewed it as part of the joy of being a father.

In her book *Parenthood by Proxy: Don't Have Them If You Won't Raise Them* (HarperCollins), best-selling author and syndicated radio-show host Dr. Laura Schlessinger candidly discusses her past negative and feminist-inspired views of marriage, family, and child rearing and how those feelings changed over time. "Not only did the rise of feminism during my tenure in college have a negative effect on my thinking about marriage and family, the constant complaining of my mother when I was growing up discouraged any positive considerations I might have had about such experiences." Schlessinger even went so far as having her tubes tied and later reversed prior to marrying. She eventually bore a child and, in the beginning, expected her husband to do half the diaper changes, feedings, and the like. But, she goes on to write, "Once Deryk was born (and he was no easy baby), I cherished and selfishly protected all these special moments. I loved changing diapers and breast-feeding him. The sense of joy from watching him giggle as I wiped his bottom is frankly indescribable, as was the sense of significance I felt watching him take nourishment from my breast. I soon gave up the fifty-fifty nonsense and we settled into doing as a team whatever needed to be done."

Quindlen's problem is like that of many other baby boomers who started families believing that they could do it all: excel in their career, raise kids, and have a life. But raising children is an enormous and time-consuming responsibility, and it's completely unrealistic and unhealthy to think that you can spend as much time at your job and career after having kids as you did before bringing kids into the picture. And if you view your children as an impediment to your career, you are not likely to savor the experience of having and raising kids. It saddens me to see how many dual-career couples compete with one another over not wanting to cut back on work and sacrifice getting ahead in their respective careers.

In her groundbreaking book *The Time Bind: When Work Becomes Home and Home Becomes Work* (Owl Books), sociologist Arlie Russell Hochschild presented her discoveries about how some employees actually prefer being at work and away from their domestic responsibilities and challenges. The real eye-openers in Hochschild's research were the choices some employees made: wealthier employees were the least interested in being at home, and few employees who could afford to do so took advantage of opportunities offered by employers (for example, paternity and maternity leave or working part-time) to spend more time at home.

Not unusual were the comments made by one employee who confessed to Hochschild to working a lot of overtime. "The more I get out of the house, the better I am. It's a terrible thing to say, but that's the way I feel. . . . I usually come to work early, just to get away from the house. When I arrive, people are there waiting. We sit, we talk, we joke." This increasing preference to avoid the home and delegate its responsibilities to outsiders was given voice in a statement once made by an acquaintance of my wife. This poster woman for feminism said, upon returning to work after a brief absence for childbirth, "I have had two days of work, and, so far, it is great. Of course, I haven't had anything to do yet, but just being in an environment where I am not defined by any of my family members is such a relief. I almost wish I could stay all day instead of leaving at 2:45!"

Stanford professor of psychiatry and behavioral sciences Laraine Zappert has spent many years with working women in her clinic, and she has also scrutinized a three-generation study of business school students. Zappert found that more than half of all moms reported "great stress" juggling work and parenting. The most common advice offered by these moms to prospective mothers was to be prepared to spend money on child care and household help, and some even advised going into debt if required!

The rise of feminism and the increased egocentrism that coincided with the generation of baby boomers reaching adulthood have sold many women a bill of goods that they can have successful full-time careers and be star parents. And, during recent decades, while men have generally become more involved at home, there has been little, if any, give on the work front. Unfortunately, few men are taking advantage of working part-time, leaving the workforce for a few years, or taking paternity leave.

The most surprising and unsettling factor to consider is that, often, a second income (from full-time work) doesn't really benefit a family much—if at all—when you factor in all of the extra expenses involved, a fact I've confirmed time and again when reviewing budgets of families in which both spouses are working full-time. In addition to the additional services (for example, child care, meals out, and household repairs and maintenance) bought when a couple is starved for time due to work, taxes can hit two-income couples hard. The largest expenditure for most families is their tax bill. Many families find that their second income ends up being taxed at a high rate when federal, state, and local taxes are tallied.

The Damage Done by Working So Much

Working too much may be the number-one untreated American addiction. Every week, I hear about yet another celebrity admitting alcohol or drug addiction and entering rehab. And you can easily find hundreds of twelve-step meetings around the country along with many other resources for helping people overcome various addictions. That's not the case for conquering workaholism, which is only beginning to be recognized as a destructive addiction. This problem has flown under the radar for so long partly because few studies have been done on those who work too much.

The Fallout from Overinvesting in Work

When people become workaholics, there are consequences. Kids don't get enough of their parents' time; physical, emotional, and mental health problems develop among all members of the family; and divorce (and even suicide) happens. I personally know more than one person who had a nervous breakdown as a result of the pressures they faced at work. And I know others whose spouse (usually the wife) walked out (most often on the husband) after feeling that the job had become more important than the marriage.

Thanks to recent studies, such as the one conducted by Professor Bryan Robinson at the University of North Carolina–Charlotte, we're now getting quantifiable proof of what should be intuitive: putting in long hours may provide financial riches, but it can leave workaholics and their families in rags emotionally. Robinson's research found that the children of workaholics suffer many of the same ills—depression, anxiety, and other emotional disorders—as the children of alcoholics. His study also found that spouses married to a workaholic felt more estranged in their marriages and less in control of their lives. In Robinson's study, just 45 percent of spouses married to workaholics remained married compared with 84 percent in marriages where no one was a workaholic.

Kids, especially young ones, benefit from time with their mom and dad. But the more we work to support car and house payments and all those toys and activities, the less time we have to be with them.

So Who's Raising Our Kids?

With moms and dads working so much, who's raising our kids? The answer: nannies, babysitters, teenage camp counselors, and the mass media—especially television. I'm not a psychologist, but I am a financial counselor and a dad. And the fact is that most of us spend more and work more than we need to. This state of affairs has long puzzled me because my best days at work don't even come close to the best days I've had with my kids.

One new mom that I know said to me, "I have to go back to work; otherwise, I'll wonder what I sacrificed in my career." That made me think, "But what about what your child has to sacrifice because you're going back to a full-time demanding career and you won't be there for most of his early years?" I didn't say that out loud, but maybe for the sake of her child, I should've taken the risk. Now I am.

Many employers, as discussed earlier in this chapter, foster a culture that rewards workaholics and encourages employees to not be home with children. A classmate of mine from Stanford Business School, Rosemary Jordano, started a business called, ironically, ChildrenFirst. ChildrenFirst was billed as a leader in backup child care, which a press release referred to as the fastest-growing segment of the "education market." In discussing her new business, which landed huge amounts of venture capital, Jordano said that she "sold the idea to law firms, banks, and corporations with a simple pitch: keeping employees at work (rather than filling in for the babysitter) was good for the bottom line." How tragic (and telling) to view parents as "filling in" for the babysitter. Keeping employees at the office more isn't better for children's "bottom line." And I'm not sure that it's better for corporations' bottom lines, either. Families aren't happier—and kids certainly aren't—when they have less time to spend together because parents work more outside the home.

Whether parents are home or not, increasingly, children are spending more time with an electronic babysitter, filling their free time with video games, television, and the Internet, among other multimedia activities. (My wife and I, I must confess, have at times been guilty of falling into the bad habit of using these sources of entertainment as a crutch when we take on too much.) Back in the mid-1960s, parents, on average, spent about *thirty hours* per week with their kids. By the turn of the century, that number was cut almost in half to *seventeen hours* weekly, according to surveys conducted by the University of Maryland. These days kids are spending in excess of *forty hours* per week watching television, playing video and computer games, and listening to pop, rock, and rap music. James Steyer, author of *The Other Parent: The Inside Story of the Media's Effect on Our Children* (Atria Books), provides a welcome dose of perspective to the situation when he says, "If another adult spent five or six hours a day with your kids, regularly exposing them to sex, violence, and rampantly commercial values, you would probably forbid that person to have further contact with them."

Schools, part-time babysitters, and video games can cover only so much time, though. A "problem" for parents consumed by work is keeping the kids busy during their summer vacation. Enter another growth business—sleep-away camps. I have to confess prior ignorance on this topic because I enjoyed my summer vacations as a child playing with kids in my neighborhood. Now I see parents of eight, nine, and ten year olds shipping their kids off to camp for the entire summer. "Each of the past twenty years, we have seen a steady 5 to 10 percent annual increase in the number of children going to sleep-away camps," says Jeffrey Solomon, executive director of the National Camp Association. According to Solomon, one of the hottest growth segments of the camper market is the increasing numbers of younger children attending: "We're seeing kids as young as four to five years old going to sleep-away camps. One of the main reasons for that is the increasing numbers of dual-career couples and people putting in more hours at work and wanting 24/7 care for their children."

What is truly horrifying is that some parents willingly send their kids off to summer camp away from home knowing that the camp won't even allow phone calls home! The logic, as it has been explained to me by the owners of these for-profit camps, is that calling home just makes kids homesick and unhappy, so the camps are really just doing what's best for the kids in not allowing phone calls.

A *New York Times* article profiled camps that allow kids to go home for the weekend. Apparently, this is another growing segment that appeals to increasing numbers of divorced parents "eager to preserve their allotted time with the child" and "working parents who have little free time during the week but want their children around when they have time off." The article quoted a Westport, Connecticut, parent of a ten-year-old camper as saying, "I'm working all week, but on weekends, I love to be with him. It's guiltless."

Not long after I read the *Times* article, I heard a group of moms complaining about the foul language and stories of teenage sexual exploits their campers had learned during the time away from home. I also ran across a Reuters article about Virginia prosecutors charging camp counselors, who were fifteen and sixteen years old, for levying admission fees on campers to view fights between ten- to twelve-year-old boys attending the camp! The fights were exposed when one camper got a broken wrist (apparently, they weren't fighting with boxing gloves) and another went home with a black eye (I guess the teenage counselors overlooked head-gear protection as well). What do you expect when teenagers are left in charge of supervising and raising kids for a summer?

Working Solutions

You *can* get too much of a good thing. Many people find that working hard pays great dividends, especially when they're lucky enough to work in a field that they've chosen and they enjoy. Gaining a sense of mastery in a given field and adding to one's knowledge base and list of accomplishments over time feel great. And who among us doesn't revel in a promotion and pay raise? But therein lies the problem in setting limits and maintaining a balance.

You can reach a tipping point with work—a point of diminishing returns. How much do you value free time to engage in your favorite activities like reading a good book, watching a movie, having dinner with friends, going for a run, or playing tennis? Are your children getting enough of your undivided attention, love, and caring? Before I dive into more specific advice about how to work less, play more, and stay fiscally fit, I want to share excerpts from some of the many notes that I've received in the past from my writing on this topic. I think you'll find many of these comments are filled with wisdom and useful perspectives:

Women say:

> It's all due to losing both of my parents at an early age, so I look at life much differently than many others. And for years I held a grudge against my mother for having all of us kids and not choosing to stay home with us, when our dad gave her that option. . . . I hope some Americans pick up on it and learn to stop spending so much money on themselves, and spend more time with their kids, because life is way too short.

> Bravo!!! Applause! Applause! I am an at-home mom and was thrilled to read your advice on investing time in people, not a thing (job). I have a BS degree in nursing, and I worked for eleven years before starting our family. (I had my first child at thirty-two.) I have never regretted being at home with them. Being part of their lives is the best investment you can make. . . . I have nieces and nephews that have been in daycare since they were six weeks old. They're in their teens now and have significant social problems. . . . When you look at the amount of teen drinking, drugs, pregnancy, and vandalism we have, a lot of that is due to lack of parental influence and example. Children are raising children. That's not how it's supposed to be! My twelve- and fourteen-year-old children still like to hold my hand when we are

shopping or crossing a street together. I think that's great! They'll be adults for a long time. I treasure every moment of childhood.

I stayed home to be with our three children. I did not go crazy— in fact, I grew in wisdom and knowledge about many things I never would have learned at work. When they were all in school, I returned to work but only working when they were in school. We were very careful how we spent our money, never buying anything on credit except our house.

As a well educated woman who is largely the product of early learning and home pre-schooling, I feel very strongly that parents should make every effort to stay at home with their children, at least until they are of school age. . . . [M]any parents are still ashamed to admit that they would rather be at home with their children for the first five or six years of their lives.

Men say:

Well, I took your advice forty-four years ago, and it worked out just as you said. . . . No, I couldn't have read you forty-four years ago, but I was lucky enough to run into an elderly man who told me to take care of God and family first, and everything else would take care of itself. He was right too. . . . My wife stayed home with the children, even though we had nothing at the beginning. We have always lived beneath our means and only collected necessary possessions, but what a life we've had! The Joneses are jealous of us!

My children are twenty-eight and thirty, and I wish that I had spent more time with them. They grew up so quickly, and I felt like a spectator. My son hit a home run in Little League, and I missed it. My daughter was in a school play, and I missed that too. I can recall these things as if they happened yesterday. I spent too much time in my small business. It's important to kids that you're there.

I lost my job nearly a year ago, and I'm optimistic of soon finding work. If the job I end up taking doesn't pay enough that it requires my wife to work full-time to stay in our present home, then we've decided that we'd rather move. It's more important to us that one of us be home for the kids.

I used to work for an aerospace firm that not only encouraged workaholics, but demanded that you work like a workaholic. I work so that I can live and have a home. I do not live to work. Most of the people that worked the way the company wanted them to are divorced and picking up the pieces of their lives. It's not worth it. . . . No job is worth high blood pressure, stroke, and/or heart attack. Family is much more important than a career. There isn't a job in the world worth losing your family over. Thanks for telling it like it is.

Initially my decision to stay at home was not by choice, as I lost my job. Over time, we decided to forego being a two-income family. My wife and I made the decision solely for the kids. You can learn to live within reduced means. There were times when having that second income would be nice, but the brief times that I went back to work made us realize the benefits of having one of us at home. The kids were really happy when we told them that I was going to be home instead of working. That was the wow factor. We always believed we were doing the right thing, but the kids' clear response really shocked us and reinforced what we were heading towards.

Finding More Time for Your Kids

Please don't get me wrong. As I've said at other points in this chapter, there's nothing inherently wrong with working hard at something. But what about your other priorities and keeping balance in your life? At what expense are you building your wealth? The United States is the world's most affluent society. So why are we working so many hours to buy all the "best things"? The best things in life—love, attention, strong family relations, friends—really can't be bought. If you've found much in this chapter that hits close to home, it's time to ask yourself one question: can you afford to be home more with your kids? Some dads and moms can't, especially if they're single parents earning modest incomes. But many parents can find ways to spend less, work less, and be with their kids more. In this section, I'm going to show you how.

One of the continuing sources of stress that pressures us to keep working so much is the rate at which we spend. So take a hard look at your expenditures over the past six months. Get out your checkbook register, credit card statements, and anything else that will help you document your spending. Determine how much you spend on clothes, restaurants, child care, cars, vacations, and so on. Ask yourself what nonessential spending you could trim. Be sure to recognize that even though a particular category like clothing is a necessity, a portion of it can be discretionary.

You and only you can make the final decision about what expenses you are most willing and able to cut. Perhaps you'd rather eat out less often instead of giving up the occasional ski outing. Discussing how, where, and why your family spends the way that it does will naturally bring up work-related topics. For example, maybe you're buying so many meals out because no one is home at a reasonable hour to start cooking dinner. The pressure to keep working is intertwined with spending.

If you're part of a dual-career household, take a hard look at the taxes you're racking up each year as well as the additional expenses you're incurring from both people working full-time. The additional costs and hassles of that second full-time job may well outweigh the increased income, and the extra earnings may be far smaller than you thought.

Consider cutting back on your work hours or switching to a more family-friendly employer—especially if you have youngsters at home. We have the rest of our lives to work but only one chance to be with our children when they're young and need us the most. If you want to consider your employment options, ask people you know for advice on good employers. You can peruse the increasing number of lists published by various magazines and Web sites of supposedly family-friendly employers. For example, *Working Mother* magazine (http://www.workingmother.com) publishes a useful annual list of family-friendly employers. The definition of *family friendly* differs among lists but is often largely based on the comprehensiveness of a cost-effective benefit package. Most lists give preference to companies offering flextime. For more employer recommendations, you can also contact the local chapter of the Society for Human Resource Management in your area. Visit their Web site at http://www.shrm.org to obtain the contact information for your local chapters.

Some people find more peace of mind with working part-time if they pay off or reduce the size of their mortgage. I've encouraged some parents to downsize to a more modest home, for example, to reduce the pressure for both people to work full-time, after assessing their financial status and their goals, both professionally and personally. Keith and Mary, for example, realized they were in over their heads once they had their third child, around the same time Keith's income dropped significantly. Despite feeling that they were going to miss out on some future appreciation in the value of their house, and even though Keith's income went back up, they decided to move to a smaller, less expensive home in the same community. "We felt a little ashamed, like we had failed in moving down, but we're less stressed [by being] able to spend less time working and thinking about work. . . . [O]thers we know are considering doing what we did."

Many—dare I say most—parents could be less busy and more involved in raising their children and simply spending time with them. Doing so requires making some difficult choices and being honest and candid with yourself, your spouse, and other family members about your priorities, needs, and wants.

If your family currently consists of you and your spouse and you don't yet have children but would like to in the future, I have two words for you: plan ahead. Adding children to the family equation is an enormous change that places all sorts of stressors on a couple. Planning ahead can go a long way toward helping you keep your heads above water financially and emotionally. Before my wife and I started our family, I made sure to structure our financial situation and obligations so that we wouldn't both be forced to work long hours. By keeping our expenses low and saving a large portion of our incomes when we were both working, my wife and I were financially able (and psychologically comfortable) with scaling back on work once we started our family. And thank goodness we were prepared because we started parenthood with a bang with the birth of twins!

The Right Way to Hire Help

Raising kids and running a household are huge responsibilities and involve tremendous time commitments, if you want to do things well. I'm not about to tell you that you should try to do everything yourself because I don't think that's the best solution for some families and because it's not the approach that I've personally taken.

If your budget and your other financial commitments and priorities allow it, by all means consider hiring some help. I suggest that you make a list of the tasks that you least enjoy doing. My list would include such tasks as oil changes on cars, general housecleaning every other week, and cleaning my home's gutters. Other people might include changing their children's diapers, picking their kids up at the bus stop, or making dinner. After you make your initial list, go through it and cross off those items that you're least comfortable delegating to someone else and the tasks that involve too much hassle or cost to delegate. The name of the game here is to free up time to spend with your kids, so give priority to delegating non-child-care items.

Where I see many families with children get into trouble is when they make sweeping decisions such as "We need a full-time live-in nanny." When that happens, numerous important aspects of child care get delegated so that parents have more time for work and nonessential activities outside the home. Think about it: would you rather have someone do a sloppy job cleaning your garage or raising your child?

Take the case of Bruce Cozadd, a 1991 graduate of Stanford's MBA program, and how he and his wife have structured their child-care schedules. Bruce searched for a company that was "not full of workaholics." But, he confesses, "Those bad genes took over, and I started climbing the ladder because it was there. At Alza Corporation, Cozadd rose to the position of chief financial officer and then chief operating officer. In order to spend more time with his family, he finally called it quits when his company was acquired and his position had him traveling much more.

Bruce and his wife, Sharon, finally set limits on the amount of child care they hire—their nanny's day ends no later than three o'clock in the afternoon. They also sit down each month, in advance, and coordinate their schedules to maximize the time they spend with their kids and each other. Although Bruce and his wife hire more child care than my wife and I would be comfortable using, I like their idea of setting limits and coordinating schedules.

One final and very important point: if you're going to hire a nanny, spend the necessary time and money and get someone who loves children and truly wants to be with your kids. You don't want someone who's going to ditch you and your kids for another job next month or next year. Take a hard look at the applicants' résumés and see what experience and interests they have in working with children. Ask applicants how long they envision staying in the job for which you're considering them. Initially, don't explain why you're asking such questions or what you're looking for, exactly. You want honest, off-the-top-of-their-head answers. Listen closely to these answers and thoroughly check references for recent work positions that applicants have held.

How Do I Know If I'm a Workaholic?

Some childless couples and single people have even greater temptations to become workaholics. Regardless of whether you have kids, as with taming any addiction, conquering the urge to overwork begins when denial ends. Below are a series of twenty questions from Workaholics Anonymous. If you answer yes to most of these questions, you probably are a workaholic.

1. Do you get more excited about your work than about family or anything else?
2. Are there times when you can charge through your work and other times when you can't?
3. Do you take work with you to bed? On weekends? On vacation?
4. Is work the activity you like to do best and talk about most?
5. Do you work more than 40 hours a week?
6. Do you turn your hobbies into money-making ventures?
7. Do you take complete responsibility for the outcome of your work efforts?
8. Have your family or friends given up expecting you on time?
9. Do you take on extra work because you are concerned that it won't otherwise get done?
10. Do you underestimate how long a project will take and then rush to complete it?
11. Do you believe that it is okay to work long hours if you love what you are doing?
12. Do you get impatient with people who have other priorities besides work?

13. Are you afraid that if you don't work hard you will lose your job or be a failure?

14. Is the future a constant worry for you even when things are going very well?

15. Do you do things energetically and competitively including play?

16. Do you get irritated when people ask you to stop doing your work in order to do something else?

17. Have your long hours hurt your family or other relationships?

18. Do you think about your work while driving, falling asleep, or when others are talking?

19. Do you work or read during meals?

20. Do you believe that more money will solve the other problems in your life?

Workaholics Anonymous

Unlike its sister organization Alcoholics Anonymous, Workaholics Anonymous has few local meetings taking place around the country. However, you may be near a town or city with a local chapter; check its Web site, http://www.workaholics-anonymous. org, for a list of current meeting locations.

Weigh your priorities and take appropriate action, including switching to an employer that doesn't encourage and reward workaholics. Start your assessment of your current employer by considering the people near the top of the organization chart. Are these "leaders" leading balanced lives? Do they have happy and fulfilling home lives, as best you can tell? Would you dare to call them role models?

Early in my career, I was working at a leading management consulting firm where the managers and partners logged many hours and were constantly on the road, away from their families. At the firm's holiday party one year, I was standing around the shrimp bowl, always a popular spot, and overheard a large group of spouses complaining about how their mates were rarely around and how their children were growing up with just one parent. I heard a lot of anger, disappointment, and resentment. These comments provided me with a new perspective on everyday events around the office. And my observations of the senior people at this consulting firm convinced me that I had no interest in staying there long-term, especially since I hoped to raise children and be an active, involved dad.

Our culture, though, too often focuses on getting ahead, promotions, and pay raises. But if you're going to make time for the important things in life, you must resist the temptation to be envious of those with loftier titles and salaries at your place of business and in your field. You can begin that process by realizing that there are no free lunches. Although some people are blessed with extraordinary talent and luck, you'll often find that the supersuccessful people in this world, with their mugs on the cover of every magazine, are workaholics. Don't emulate these workaholics to get "ahead." Perhaps the news media should cover the realities of the personal lives and emotional well-being of these career superstars as thoroughly as they tally their business and financial success. Then we'd have a realistic perspective of the rewards and consequences of chasing after capitalism's spoils.

I met Dr. Laird Stuart during my years living in San Francisco, and he was probably one of the best preachers I've known. He did an outstanding job combining religious teachings with practical, real-world issues that people struggle with. One morning, he was especially on his game when he said, "We all lose our bearings sometimes." He continued with the story of baseball player Matt Williams, who at the time was playing for the San Francisco Giants. Matt Williams worked to get traded, and agreed to less money, to Phoenix where his family and kids are. "Anyone who will take less money to be with his children has got his bearings," said Dr. Stuart.

Unlike Matt Williams, basketball legend Michael Jordan didn't put his family first, even though he clearly could afford to do so. Comments and quotes from Jordan in 1994 and again in 1999 when he "retired" from basketball cited his supposed desire to spend more time with his family. But after retiring from his playing career in 1999, and despite being worth hundreds of millions of dollars, Jordan signed on with the Washington Wizards basketball team in Washington, D.C., far away from his family and home in the Chicago area. Not only did he take on a demanding management role and an ownership interest in the team, but he also eventually returned to playing full-time. With children who were nine, eleven, and thirteen years old at the time, Jordan and his wife filed for divorce in 2002. When interviewed by Reuters, Jordan said, "I come out, do my job and focus on what's enjoyable for me, which is playing the game of basketball." A young man on a Yahoo! message board said in response to this comment, "Which is his game, not his kids or marriage. Nice priorities Michael. I once actually admired you."

Although there's far less excuse for wealthy people not to cut back on workaholic schedules, few do it. In fact, it's so unusual that, when it happens, it actually makes news. Tom Bloch resigned as CEO of H&R Bloch to become a teacher in a Missouri middle school. He had recognized that his hectic CEO schedule interfered with his top priority, which he said was his wife and two sons. He added that he didn't want to look back on his life and say, "Gee, you had an opportunity to play a bigger role in your children's lives and didn't take it." Well said, Tom Bloch!

Over the years, I've seen many people with modest incomes make the decision to fit work into their lives rather than continuing to try to fit their lives into their work. So often, though, people twist and contort their lives and priorities to meet the perceived expectations and demands of their bosses and employers. Fitting work into the rest of your life often involves choosing employers and even careers that provide you the flexibility and ability to accomplish your personal and family goals.

MISALIGNED INVESTMENT MIND-SETS: THE HERD FOLLOWER AND INFORMATION JUNKIE

In the late 1990s, Harry, who had never paid much attention to the stock market, loaded up on technology stocks. We were entering the information age, and the new economy and the companies that were driving it like Dell, Cisco Systems, JDS Uniphase, Amazon.com, eBay, American Online, Yahoo!, and Lucent, were growing fast. For years, Harry had heard of more and more people seemingly making millions off this sure-win trend. The only problem was that Harry hadn't a clue about how to value a company and its stock, and he also didn't recognize the risk of recession. When technology stocks crashed in the early 2000s, Harry became so frightened that he no longer invested *any* money in stocks after losing so much. He retreated into cash but then became tempted to try his hand at real estate since that avenue provided what he believed was more direct control over his investment.

Paul is a marriage and family counselor by profession. Despite being far more of an expert than the rest of us when it comes to understanding psychology, when the stock market crashed, Paul began coming to terms with his own relationship with money and the psychological obstacles he faced as an investor. "I got overconfident with my stock picking. Some of my stocks soared, and I met with success in a previous company where I was responsible for choosing investment funds, one of which returned 90 percent in a year," says Paul. When the market crashed, Paul was "psychologically devastated" as he lost about two-thirds of the money he'd saved over the prior ten years.

Paul's overconfidence and the pain he felt losing money were wake-up calls. Fortunately for Paul, his awareness of the importance of nonfinancial issues (like emotional and mental health concerns) and his conversations with others about this helped him bounce back from the hit and gradually institute a prudent approach to investing. Most other people (like Harry, for example) aren't so fortunate. They literally can't recognize or work their way around the obstacles that stand in the way of investing success. This chapter will discuss how to identify the impediments to developing sound investing habits and what you can do to stack the investing odds in your favor.

Redefining Investing Success

Just as with dealing with pressures and purchasing decisions in a consumer society, raising children, or pursuing a career, "success" at personal investing is somewhat in the eye of the beholder. In my work as a financial counselor and lecturer, I've come to define a successful investor as someone who, with a minimal commitment of time, develops an investment plan to accomplish important financial and personal goals and earns returns comparable to the market averages.

I know people who view investing as a hobby. Some belong to investing clubs, other people simply enjoy reading about personal-financial matters, and still others relish the time spent researching and tracking various investments. We all have hobbies. One of mine is researching and learning about personal health issues. I consider my time spent reading about nutrition, exercise, and other health-related concerns to be a hobby because I enjoy doing it and talking with others who share a similar interest. I have no doubt that I benefit from my hobby (and I have evidence to back it up).

I raise the example of one of my own hobbies to illustrate a broader concern about hobbies crossing a line and becoming obsessions. In my own case, what if I spent numerous hours every week poring over medical journals and reports, worrying about the latest conflicting studies and constantly tinkering with my personal health practices, and in the process I was neglecting my family, friends, and professional commitments? In that case, most sensible people would consider my behavior to be problematic and indicative of an obsession or fixation that far surpasses the "hobby" level. However, it's not just about how much time you spend at something but also about the *consequences* of that time spent.

Too often, I see people spending many hours obsessing over their investments. To make matters worse, these people typically end up doing a far worse job with their investments because they trade too much and make more emotional, knee-jerk decisions. (I'll delve more fully into these issues later in this chapter.) If you consider investing to be your hobby, ask your loved ones and friends to honestly tell you if your perceived hobby has grown into something far more problematic. If you're afraid to raise the subject because of what you expect the answer to be, then you probably already have all the information you need to objectively answer your concerns.

Establishing Return Expectations

One of the reasons that people develop and continue detrimental investing habits is that many investors have unrealistic return expectations. After going through years of higher education—and incurring the often humongous associated costs—and being out in the working world for a while, it's no wonder that so many people (especially men) resort to various schemes to "get rich quicker" than can be normally and reasonably accomplished from investing. Mixing in all the media stories of entrepreneurs becoming multimillionaires from stock offerings also adds to the feeling that one must pick up the pace to become "rich" now.

Stocks, historically, have produced returns averaging about 9 to 10 percent per year. Some people find that kind of depressing because they want to quickly double their money and then double it again so that they feel that they have some hope of retiring. That's why financial-market and magazine reports that focus on high-flying stocks are so dangerously tempting. Why wait seven or eight years for your investment to double, which is how long it takes with a 9 to 10 percent annual return, when some stocks double or more in less than a year? Well, the reason, quite simply, is that risky investment schemes often crash and burn and regular savings and steady and moderate returns produce awesome long-term outcomes.

Though some people are able to start their own businesses or achieve high incomes from their work, the best chance for most of us to build the wealth that we desire to accomplish our personal and financial goals is through systematic saving and investing. Consider that through the miracle of compounding, for every $2,500 per year that you can invest in a tax-deferred account returning an average of 10 percent per year, you'll have about $220,000 in twenty years and $1.7 million in forty years.

Investing in real estate produces similar long-term returns as those realized by investing in stocks. Some real estate investors are able to do better. Further, the most successful small-business owners generally earn the highest investment returns. The focus of this chapter, however, is for people who invest in stocks and other securities that are actively traded in the financial markets because it is in this venue that people make so many avoidable mistakes.

Common Investing Obstacles

Just about everyone I've ever met has made avoidable investment blunders. The key word here is *avoidable*. I'm not about to tell you that I have some secret system that guarantees 100 percent of your investments will do what you hope and expect them to do. (I'll leave that to the late-night infomercial hucksters and the most unscrupulous of brokers out there.) My goal here is to help you identify the self-defeating investing behaviors we all are prone to and then discuss the best remedies for minimizing your chances of making such mistakes and how you can maximize your chances of earning healthy returns.

Getting Swept Up by Euphoria

Some investors, feeling strength and safety in numbers, are lured into buying hot stocks and sectors after major price increases.

We find it reassuring to buy into something that's going up and gaining accolades. The danger in following such a path is that you're buying into investments that are selling at inflated and soon-to-be-deflated prices. Sometimes entire stock markets (Japan in the late 1980s) get overheated, whereas at other moments specific industries are driven to excess valuations (Internet and technology stocks in the late 1990s). A herd mentality can take over at such times, as well as performance envy. We hear about and know others who seem to be getting rich easily, and this is especially infuriating when some of these people aren't likable or all that bright!

If you take a step back and examine these soaring stock and sector situations with an open mind, you can come to the conclusion that the higher prices rise, the greater the risk that the investment will soon fall. But typical investors don't think that way. Robert Shiller, professor of economics at Yale University, conducted a survey of Japanese investors and found that just 14 percent were expecting a major correction at that market's peak in 1989, when Japanese stocks were selling at outrageous price/earnings (P/E) multiples (the level of stock prices relative to corporate profits). By the mid-1990s, after most of the correction had taken place, when the Japanese market was down 60+ percent from its peak and selling at *less risky* levels (versus the inflated prices of the late 1980s), far more investors (32 percent) were expecting a crash.

Investors, and people in general, tend to place too much emphasis on recent events. Before September 11, 2001, most people went about their daily lives and didn't think about terrorism. In the days and months after September 11, far more people thought and worried about the risk of terrorists striking again. The same simplistic thinking occurs with investments.

Stocks and sectors that are doing well are usually expected to continue to perform. Likewise, many investors flee falling investments. Investors tend to get more optimistic as prices rise and increasingly pessimistic as prices fall. More often than not, investors make simplistic extrapolations of the past and fail to research and do their homework. This is why many studies have found that the average investor has a tendency to buy high and sell low and actually ends up earning returns lower than the market averages.

Overconfidence

Many people are overconfident in their own abilities and knowledge, especially relative to others. Studies have shown, for example, that about 80 percent of drivers rate themselves as "above average."

In a study titled "Boys Will Be Boys: Gender, Overconfidence, and Common Stock Investment" (published in the *Quarterly Journal of Economics*), Brad Barber and Terrance Odean found that men tend to be more overconfident, trade more, and earn lower returns than women. Their analysis of tens of thousands of brokerage accounts demonstrated that "men trade 45 percent more than women and earn annual risk-adjusted net returns that are 1.4 percent less than those earned by women. These differences are more pronounced between single men and single women; single men trade 67 percent more than single women and earn annual risk-adjusted net returns that are 2.3 percent less than those earned by single women."

Financial newsletter writers, book authors, and even some periodicals mislead investors into thinking that picking their own stocks is the best approach to investing in the market. Individual stock investors should be clear as to why they're investing in individual stocks. If your primary motivation is that you think you can earn higher returns than a money manager running a mutual fund, calculate what your actual returns, net of all trading fees and after taxes, have been each year over the past five years. Now compare your returns with those of the relevant market averages and those earned by comparable mutual funds. If you can consistently beat the averages and the pros, you're an anomaly and in the wrong profession. You could be making really big bucks as a money manager.

Another mistake common to individual stock–picking investors is to be overly optimistic about a company's future earnings, which is the single most important stock-price determinant in the long-term. When investors fall in love with a company and its stock, they tend to lose sight of the harsh realities of competition and economic downturns.

Paul's challenge was that his early investment success in a strong stock market led him to believe that he had the magic investing touch, which caused him to trade excessively and take risks. When the market reversed course, losses came in droves. "I realized that if I was going to be a stock trader, I had to work at it full-time and be prepared anxiety-wise to handle it. I thought that I really had it all figured out. Now, I know I don't," says Paul. He is typical of investors who fail to do adequate research and incorrectly chalk up their gains to their own genius (rather than simply being in the stock market while prices were rising), which can lead to investing in things that they don't really understand.

Whitney has a Harvard MBA, but his stock picks in the late 1990s, despite a soaring market, were faring poorly. "I'm embarrassed to say that I was buying stocks solely on the basis of friend's tips or using products that I liked," says Whitney. For example, Whitney's Apple computer had a Global Village modem that he liked, so he bought stock in the company, which soon went bankrupt. "I didn't do my research," says Whitney, adding, "I was busy with my work as the executive director of a nonprofit. I was being greedy trying to select small companies in the hopes they'd be the next Microsoft so that I could realize big gains quickly. It was exciting investing in risky stocks."

When I interviewed Whitney in 1999, he was just gushing about Dell. He'd even call me and go on and on about how wonderful a company and stock it was. At the time, shares were around fifty dollars, but eventually plunged below twenty dollars during the bear market, taking Whitney and many other latecomers with it. Dell stock has since recovered but is still not back to its prior heights.

One last important point on overconfidence: when investors turn to mutual funds, they have a tendency to make the same types of investing errors that they do with individual stocks. Too often, investors put their money into actively managed funds (and sometimes narrowly focused industry "sector" funds) that are currently near the top of the short-term performance charts rather than choosing low-cost index funds that will outperform the highfliers in the long run.

Control Issues

I know well from my years as a financial planner, lecturer, and writer that there are some people who have control issues with regards to their investments. These folks have great difficulty turning their money over to someone else to manage, as you do, for example, when you invest in a mutual fund. In my experience, such investors prefer investing in real estate and individual stocks of their own choosing.

The rise of the Internet and online trading has created the illusion of more control and involvement. Now investors can watch every little movement of their favorite stocks and jump in and out with a quick couple of clicks on their computer's mouse. The advent of the Internet and growth of online trading capabilities spawned a whole new generation of short-term (sometimes, even day) traders. Interestingly, in other parts of our lives, a lack of self-control is readily acknowledged as leading to problems (like overeating, overspending, or overworking). But most folks have a harder time seeing how the quick and easy access to our investment money, which is highly valued by some investors, can cause problems due to our lack of control and lead to overtrading.

Panic and Emotional Selling

For inexperienced or nervous investors, bailing out when it appears that an investment isn't going to be profitable and enjoyable can be tempting. Some investors run to dump falling investments precisely at the times when they should be doing the reverse—buying more. For example, in 2002 and early 2003, the U.S. stock market endured several periods of heavy selling. After peaking in 2000, the market had already sustained a significant decline and then plunged further in the first week that it was open following the September 11, 2001, terrorist attacks. The events of September 2001 helped drag down the economy, corporate profits plummeted, and then the war in Iraq started. So plenty of negative news was floating around, and it was too much to bear for many investors who bailed out of falling stocks. Investors who sold at the lows of 2002–2003, though, missed out on a 50 percent rally within the next year.

As a financial counselor, I can usually tell when a stock market decline is close to running its course. I'll see a peak in calls and e-mails coming in from investors worried whether they should sell before it gets worse. The worries almost always stem from things they've heard on the news: on the radio, television, online articles, you name it. Most of what the general news media report on—murders, major accidents, bankruptcies, and so on—is negative and frankly depressing. And the financial media often follow the same prescription—sensational reports "sell." A steady diet of that is enough to turn you off to investing (and perhaps life in general) during difficult times.

The *Journal of the American Medical Association* conducted a survey of the impact of the 9/11 events and feelings of posttraumatic stress. The study found that the people who were the most distressed, not surprisingly, were those who watched the most television. This confirms my experience as a financial counselor: the people most upset by stock market declines and the negative happenings surrounding such falls were those who listened to the most media reports.

Anxiety and Overmonitoring

I've seen time and time again that investors who are the most anxious about their investments and most likely to make impulsive trading decisions are the ones who watch their holdings closely, especially those who monitor prices daily. The investment world seems so risky and fraught with pitfalls that some people believe that closely watching an investment can help alert them to impending danger. "The constant tracking is not unlike the attempt to relieve anxiety by fingering worry beads. Yet, paradoxically, it can increase emotional distress because it requires a constant state of vigilance," says psychologist Dr. Paul Minsky.

Investors who monitor their holdings closely trade more and, not surprisingly, earn worse returns (see the section earlier in this chapter called "Overconfidence"). When such investors or traders start losing money, their judgment actually gets even worse. In a landmark study by Dr. William Gehring and Dr. Adrian Willoughby of the University of Michigan, researchers analyzed what happens when people make risky choices in gambling games and lose. Subjects who suffer such losses experience heightened brain activity symptomatic of distress, which causes them to be more likely to make knee-jerk and irrational decisions to try to quickly win the money back. Unfortunately, the Internet has aggravated the problem by enabling the worst offenders to track stock prices and news releases by the minute.

To add insult to injury (and give you yet another good reason to trade less), researchers have found a clear link between daily tracking of investments and poor mental health. A study published in the *Journal of Social and Clinical Psychology* reported that those who follow the stock market closely generally had the worst problems with pessimism and depression. Researchers believe that these results are due to the fact that such investors are closely monitoring a situation that *they have no control over,* and when things go against them, they get demoralized. Remember the saying "Ignorance is bliss." I'm not advocating sticking your head in the sand and ignoring your investments, but if you follow every little up and down, the down times will inevitably wear on you.

What the study didn't highlight is the damage done beyond the investor's poor mental health. Most of us don't have much free time, and if so much time is being devoted to tracking investments, the investors' personal relationships, family members, and friends pay the price too. In my counseling work, I frequently heard about these broader problems. Typical is the following complaint one woman made to me: "Every day, my husband spends many hours on the Internet following his individual stocks. He says we have been doing well, but we never go anywhere or do anything together. This type of investing worries me. What's your perspective?"

Investing in individual stocks requires extensive research and time, if you want to do it well. However, as I've demonstrated, when taken to an extreme, the time and energy some folks expend watching their investments can negatively impact their emotional and mental well-being, their personal relationships, and, in the cruelest twist of all, the performance of that portfolio they are lavishing so much attention on.

Here's a test to see if such behavior has become problematic for you or someone you care about. For a period of one week (Monday through Friday), keep track of how much total time is spent monitoring stocks, including time reading about stocks, looking at stock prices, watching the financial networks, and conversing with other investors, including online chat groups. Now compare this total to the amount of time spent during these days socializing with friends (work time doesn't count). If the first number comes close to or actually exceeds the second number, that's a red flag.

STOCK MARKET CONTESTS

While I'm all in favor of educational endeavors, I'm disappointed by the vast majority of the stock market contests that I see (some of which require entry fees). Many of them claim to be educational, but I would beg to differ because they don't teach people about the best and most realistic ways to invest. Most of these contests are way too short in duration, such as a mere three months. One newspaper editor's justification to me on this count was, "We considered having it run for a year, like another newspaper does, but they have found that people lose interest or forget that they entered." In addition to focusing people on short-term results, these contests are won by people who take extreme risks in their selections and get lucky. In essence, these contests are more like a lottery than a true forum for sharpening investment skills.

Getting Weighed Down by Anchoring

Another problem that some investors have is getting fixated on a particular price for an investment. Often, this point of stubborn fascination is the original price that they paid for an investment (or it could be the value of an investment when they inherited it). When investors fall into this trap, they can lose their ability to objectively assess the merits or shortcomings of an investment.

The price per share that a stock trades for, in and of itself, is completely and utterly meaningless unless you know the company's earnings per share and other important financial information. A surprising number of investors, however, leap to erroneous assumptions about the attractiveness, or lack thereof, of a company's stock on the basis of the price per share. Some investors shy away from stocks that trade at higher prices per share, concerned that they may be overpriced.

Companies knowingly take advantage of this human tendency by using stock splits to entice investors to buy their stock. This was a major mechanism by which grossly overpriced technology and Internet stocks continued to attract more investors. The wildly popular Cisco Systems, for example, split five times alone in the latter half of the 1990s! These decisions enabled the company to keep the stock price much less than $100 per share and attractive to far more investors. Had the splits not occurred, the stock would've been trading at nearly $1,500 per share. Investors who snapped up the stock in late 1999 and early 2000 were paying an outrageous price/earnings multiple of more than 200. (During "normal" times, the overall stock market sells at a P/E of about 15 to 20, whereas fast-growing companies typically sell at a P/E of about 30 to 50.) The very next year, 2001, the economy tanked, and Cisco's earnings took a huge hit—dropping by about half. Cisco's stock got hammered— plunging nearly 87 percent in just a little more than a year.

Internet darlings Yahoo! and Amazon.com also managed their stock prices in similar fashion during frenzied buying of their shares in the late 1990s. At its peak in 2000, Yahoo! reached $125 per share, but it would've been about $1,500 in the absence of its numerous splits in the latter 1990s. At its peak, its P/E was an astounding 521! Yahoo!'s stock plunged nearly 97 percent during the bear market. Amazon.com's stock price reached $113 in 1999, but in the absence of its stock splits, the price would've been $1,356 per share. Amazon's P/E ratio was ∞ because the company had no earnings! Its stock plunged 95 percent during the bear market.

Placing Trust in Salespeople

Some investors assume knowledge, competence, and ethics on the part of hired advisers if the person has an important-sounding title such as vice president or certified financial planner, dresses the part, and occupies plush, high-cost office space. But the fact of the matter is that such accoutrements can just as often be leading indicators of a salesperson, and not an unbiased adviser, earning big commissions and fees siphoned from investors' dollars. Additionally, placing too much trust in an expert can lead to laziness when investors spend too little time monitoring their investments and making decisions without doing independent research. Figuring that Joe Financial Consultant is an expert, some investors blindly follow him straight into bad investments (for the investor, not the commissioned agent) without ever questioning recommendations or analyzing their investments' performance over time.

Mary was an older widow living on a modest fixed income who was drawn to a bank salesperson pitching an annuity with a high initial "teaser" interest rate. She developed symptoms of anxiety in the form of sleep problems because of buyer's remorse. She was too proud and ashamed to ask for help. Mary didn't need the tax shelter (and the associated high fees) of an annuity, and she would not likely keep her money in the annuity long enough for any small tax benefits to make up for its relatively high fees.

Nick and Joyce had two young children and knew that they needed to buy some life insurance, but they had never gotten around to it. One day, a salesperson, who was a friend of Nick, called the couple at home and pitched them some costly whole-life policies (which combine life insurance with a low-return investment account). Without doing any research or comparison shopping, Nick and Joyce each bought a policy. Due to the high costs, they got far less insurance coverage than they really needed, and they paid nearly triple what they should have for the type of policy they bought because they failed to shop around.

Preferring Pundits' Perspectives

Another huge obstacle that may be standing squarely in the way of your investment success is the belief that you must find a guru—or two or three—to turn to for the latest prognostications on the financial markets. Many of these pundits appeal to our fears and greed. Some people believe that they need some self-styled expert to predict what will happen with the economy, foreign trade, interest rates, the value of specific investments— you name it—in the weeks, months, and years ahead. Some folks take it even further: they look to these pundits to tell them not only what to buy but also when to buy and sell it.

Unfortunately, the news media have no shortage of nicely dressed, articulate lads and ladies willing to spout off and make predictions. This fascination with talking heads gets people on the air, and it gets many viewers to stay tuned in. But months and years down the road, few will remember who predicted what. There's little if any accountability, and that's the beauty of the game for the market gurus. Nearly every study that I've seen of economists' and pundits' predictions demonstrates that their track records aren't any better (and often are worse), on average, than one you'd expect to build by chance (throwing darts at a dartboard).

Holding the Losers and Cutting the Winners Loose

Whereas some investors realize that they can't withstand losses and sell at the first signs of trouble, other investors find it so painful and unpleasant to sell a losing investment that they'll continue holding a poorly performing investment despite its lousy future prospects. The late Amos Tversky, a Stanford psychology professor, and Daniel Kahneman of Princeton University documented how people find accepting a given loss more than twice as painful when compared with the emotion associated with a gain of equal magnitude.

Because most investors find losses more painful to accept compared with the pleasure they get from gains, they often take more risk to avoid losses. Most investors also prefer to lock in a small gain rather than risk losing it while waiting for a larger gain. These tendencies can cause investors to hold on to their losers and to sell their winners far too early because they don't want the pain that comes with realizing a loss. University of California professor Terrance Odean conducted a study of brokerage accounts and found that the winning stocks that people sold greatly outperformed the losers that they held on to.

According to investment manager Ken Fisher, when investments fall, some people hold on, thinking it's too late; then, when the market comes back, they have an overwhelming desire to get out at the point where they break even. "Even though there can be tax benefits, investors like to avoid having to recognize a loss and the humiliation that comes with it," says Fisher.

When you sell and actually realize a loss, it's seen as admitting to your poor investment decision, an act that can be personally humbling. Other folks, including your tax preparer and spouse, will see what you did as well.

Attachment

Just as we get attached to people, places, and things, some investors' judgment may be clouded due to attachment to an investment. Even if an investor makes the decision to sell an investment based on a sound and practical assessment, their attachment to it can derail the process, causing them to refuse to part with it at the current fair market value. Attachment can be especially problematic and paralyzing with inherited assets. Over the years, I've worked with many clients (and family members) who had great difficulty being objective with and letting go of inherited investments.

Inertia

Inertia is also a problem for some people. It wasn't unusual for me to work with clients who had accumulated tens or hundreds of thousands of dollars in checking accounts. One client even came to me with $1.5 million in his *checking account!* In nearly all of these cases, the person had either inherited the money or accumulated it through savings from his or her work. Clients who amassed their savings from work income, including the fellow with $1.5 million in cash, were often fearful of selecting an investment that might fall in value. These people knew how long and hard they had had to work for their money, and they didn't want to lose any of it.

Failing to Consider the Big Picture

When I first started my work as a financial planner and counselor, I was surprised at how often I'd meet with clients who had excess cash in a low-interest money-market fund or savings account while they carried high-cost debt like auto loans and credit card balances. I was able to convince many of these people to pay down the high-cost debt after I showed them how much they could save or make by doing so.

Likewise, I found that investors who preferred individual stocks would fret when one of their holdings fell, and they wouldn't examine their overall portfolio's performance. Too frequently, such investors would dump a stock currently in the hole because they'd dwell on that stock's large decline and overlook how little impact this one holding had on their overall portfolio.

When purchasing a new investment, many people fail to consider their overall asset allocation. Typically, they read an article somewhere or get a tip from a colleague and then wind up buying a recommended investment. In addition to not having done sufficient homework, investing in this fashion leads to a hodgepodge of a portfolio that's often not properly diversified. Failure to make an overall plan usually leads to a plan for failure, not success.

Wanting to be loyal team players, other folks fail to consider the big picture and overinvest in employer stock. This strategy is particularly dangerous because if a company falls on hard times, it can lead to not only the loss of a job but also the loss of retirement assets when the stock takes a permanent nosedive.

Investing Solutions

Conquering bad investing habits can easily translate into hundreds of thousands more dollars (perhaps millions for high-income earners) for an individual by the time he or she reaches retirement. Once you can identify and overcome the roadblocks I discussed earlier in this chapter, staying on the right path is relatively simple if you can remember a few basic points. The best investors have a simple plan, do their homework, and maintain a long-term perspective. They also understand the vital importance of keeping the fees and taxes that they pay to a minimum.

Investing is clearly more complicated than just setting your goals and choosing solid investments. Awareness and understanding of the cerebral and emotional issues covered earlier in this chapter will maximize your chances for investing success. So, in addition to considering your goals in a traditional sense before investing (identifying when you want to retire, how much of your kids' college costs you desire to pay, and so on), you should also consider what you want and don't want to get from the process of investing. Is it a hobby or simply another of life's tasks, such as maintaining your home? Do you desire the intellectual challenge of picking your own stocks, or would you be content with entrusting some of those decisions to others? Deciding how you feel about these issues will shape your approach to managing your investments. Don't just ponder these questions on your own. Discuss them with family members too—after all, you're all going to have to live with the investment decisions and results.

Develop an overall allocation plan among various investments. After you develop your allocation plan, stick with it. Don't make knee-jerk decisions to change it based on the latest hot sectors. Keeping in mind that the goal of an asset-allocation plan is to develop a mix of stock and bond holdings to accomplish your objectives, I know of no better way to accomplish that, with relatively minimal effort, than to invest in diversified mutual funds. These funds allow you to forgo the difficult and stressful process of picking stocks and deciding how much to place in various industries. If you're investing partly for fun and you enjoy researching and tracking individual stocks, earmark a portion—perhaps no more than, say, 20 percent of your money—for individual stocks. By all means, do your homework to identify good companies to invest in, but after you've identified a dozen or so companies in different industries, buy 'em and hold 'em for the long haul.

As another component of your new (or refocused) long-term mind-set, if you're going to invest in individual stocks or market sectors, de-emphasize or avoid stocks and sectors at the top of the performance charts. Think back to the last time you went bargain shopping for a consumer item. You looked for value, not high prices. For example, if you took the time to research and identify "value stocks" in the late 1990s, you likely found some terrific buys, as the herds were ignoring many solid offerings to chase after popular growth stocks.

As you research and follow your investments, restrict your diet of financial information and advice. Quality is far more important than quantity. If you invest in diversified mutual funds, then you really don't need to examine your fund's performance more than once *per year*. This recommendation may surprise you, especially if you're an Internet-tracking junkie suffering from investment-information overload, but I assure you that I'm serious. An ideal time to review your funds is when you receive their annual reports. Although many investors track their funds on a daily or weekly basis, far fewer bother to read the funds' annual reports. Doing so will help you keep a long-term perspective and gain some understanding as to why your funds are performing as they are and how they're doing in comparison to major market averages.

When you invest in stocks and bonds, you must accept the fact that there will be short-term declines, sometimes substantial drops, in your investments' values. This is never enjoyable. A simple solution is to not track your investment values closely. Examine your returns over longer periods (years, not months) to help keep the proper perspective. During difficult times, minimize your exposure to financial coverage on the news. Tuning in to the financial cable networks and listening to commentators dwell on the carnage around them on the trading floor won't encourage you to hold on to or add to your investments.

The key to effectively dealing with events that negatively impact your investment portfolio is not to panic. Slow down and pull back from stressful situations and news before making decisions. As with everything in life, recognize what you can and cannot control. Don't waste your time or energy by closely following things that you have no control over. I'm a big fan of the "Serenity Prayer." It might help you to post this someplace where you'll see it daily, especially if you try to exert too much control over every little aspect of your investment portfolio, or your life in general:

Grant me the Serenity to accept
The things I cannot change,
Courage to change the things I can,
And Wisdom to know the difference.

I really like company investment plans, such as 401(k)s, that limit people to trading only a few times a year (once per quarter is common). Instituting a similar restriction for your own personal investment accounts can prevent you from making emotional, impulsive reactions to current bad (or good) news.

Difficult times and market declines will undoubtedly occur, so be sure to invest new money on a regular basis, such as monthly or quarterly (known as dollar cost averaging), so that you'll benefit from buying during market downswings. Also, consider investing in highly diversified, less volatile mutual funds of mutual funds (such as Vanguard's LifeStrategy funds) that hold several funds investing in stocks worldwide as well as bonds.

If you're the type of investor who is unable to mentally and emotionally withstand the volatility of riskier growth-oriented investments such as stocks and hold on through market declines, you may be better off not investing in such vehicles to begin with. Recognize, though, the "risk" you're taking by placing all of your money in low-return investments like CDs: you'll have to work more years and save more money to reach your financial goals or accept a lower standard of living.

Assessing Your Current Portfolio

With all this talk of holding on for the long haul, don't think that there aren't times when selling is appropriate. In fact, if you've been holding investments that seem to be doing poorly over an extended period of time, I'd advise you to closely examine the situation. Try to determine why they've done so poorly. If a given investment is down because similar ones are also in decline, and the long-term fundamentals still hold, then so should you.

However, if there's something inherently wrong with the investment in question, such as high fees or poor management, take the loss and make doing so more palatable by remembering two things. First, if it's a non-retirement-account investment, keep in mind that losses help reduce your income taxes. Second, consider the "opportunity cost" of continuing to keep your money in a lousy investment—what kind of future return could that money be providing you if you switched to a better investment?

A useful way to evaluate your portfolio once a year or every few years is to imagine that everything that you currently own is sold. Ask yourself whether you'd choose to go out and buy the same investments again. This is an especially good question to ask yourself if you own a lot of stock in the company you work for. Are your reasons still valid for holding your investments?

When assessing your current holdings, be careful that you don't dump a particular investment just because it's in what will turn out to be a temporary slump. But remember: my definition of temporary is one to two years, not months or days. Even the best mutual fund managers have periods as long as a year or two during which they underperform. (Sometimes this happens when the fund manager's style of investing is out of favor for the time being.)

Conquering Your Stock-Investing Fears

Helping people overcome their stock investing fears and worries, whether they were the product of a lack of experience or a bad experience, was one of my challenges as a financial adviser. When we're young, we learn (sometimes the hard way) not to touch a hot stove or to lean back in our chair. Self-inflicted pain from easily avoidable behavior is a powerful teacher. Therefore, after a major market slide like the one we had in the early 2000s, it's understandable on one level why some people decided that they don't want to have anything to do with stocks. In the years leading up to the market peak in the spring of 2000, investors snapped up stocks and shunned bonds. Three years later, many investors were doing just the opposite—dumping their beaten-down stocks and buying more highly priced bonds. Opening up our investment statements personalized the pain we'd already experienced when listening to the daily news reports of falling stock prices.

It takes courage (some might call it foolishness and stupidity) to buy stocks in the face of war, terror alerts, talk of smallpox, sagging retail sales, and more corporate layoffs and profit disappointments. Few investors had the constitution to buy stocks after such a brutal bear market (U.S. stocks slid about 50 percent over three years). Those who buy after such a significant drop are rewarded—and sometimes without having to wait for very long.

That's why I say that if you're uncomfortable with investing and you're watching and listening to excessive amounts of negative, hyped news, the first thing you need to do is change your media diet. To be a successful long-term stock market investor, you must be reasonably optimistic. Much of what's in the news is bad news, and the more of that you subject yourself to and dwell on, the more fearful and unwilling you're going to be to invest. Successful investors see the glass as half full rather than half empty.

My favorite stock market strategy for skittish investors is to buy the most conservative stock funds you can find that will join in any future appreciation but not get clobbered if more tough times lay ahead. Participate in the upside, but limit your downside. Among the safer stock mutual funds, buy value-oriented funds from the more conservative fund-management companies like Vanguard and Dodge & Cox. Value stock funds, such as Fidelity Equity Income, Masters Select Value, and Vanguard's various value index funds invest in shares that are selling at a low price relative to the intrinsic value of the company.

Buy good, balanced funds, such as Dodge & Cox Balanced, Fidelity's Freedom funds, T. Rowe Price Balanced, and Vanguard's LifeStrategy funds, instead of holding stocks and bonds separately. Such funds offer the feeling of a smoother ride as stocks and bonds diversify and soften the ups and downs in a portfolio.

Many people, of course, are not comfortable with investing on their own, and you may still not be at ease enough to pick from the short list of funds that I've provided. If you lack the confidence to invest on your own and you're attracted to the idea of hiring someone to help you, first work at gaining a basic investing education. How can you possibly assess the competence and discern the agenda of someone that you're considering hiring if you don't have at least a working knowledge of the topic yourself? Learn the jargon and how to evaluate investments by reading up on the topic. I'm a fan of good books, which are free from the inevitable conflicts of interest that come from advertising. Also, seek independent second opinions before acting on an adviser's recommendations. Any financial adviser upset with you for seeking a second opinion isn't someone you should be working with.

Lessons from Company-Stock Price Collapses in Retirement Plans

You've surely heard tales of companies engaged in layoffs simultaneously experiencing earnings declines and plummeting stock prices. In the worst cases, employees who've invested significant chunks of money in their firm's stock end up losing their jobs and holding deflated retirement plans. Although you can't completely eliminate your anxieties about job losses and stock-price plunges, you can take action to minimize the fallout from future corporate disasters.

When considering a job offer, thoroughly review the company's benefit package, especially their retirement-plan investments.

Be wary of plans that require you to hold too much company stock for too long (years). I don't have a problem with investing some money—say, 10 or 20 percent of your account—in your employer's equity. But unless you can truly withstand the risk, I'd stay away from plans and employers that require more significant amounts than that to be held in company stock. This isn't about showing your loyalty and faith in the company; it's about avoiding a foolish and dangerous lack of diversification. No one in the executive suite is going to shed a tear about you losing your job and retirement dreams. And even if they did share your sorrow, it's not going to bring your job and investment money back. Protect yourself and diversify. Here are some things to keep in mind:

- Seek out independent reviews of the investment choices in the company's retirement plan. Give preference to broadly diversified mutual funds and shun individual stocks and sector (or industry) funds.
- Try evaluating the company culture and value system and the management team's ethics. It's natural to avoid asking tougher questions when you're trying to get a job offer, so save the more difficult queries for after you secure an offer.
- Take the time to speak with numerous people at your prospective employer. Ask them what they like and don't like about the company and what kinds of people fit in best and what types don't. Also, inquire about the ethical standards, expectations, and behaviors of senior management.
- Take off your rose-colored glasses and be open to the possibility that the company isn't the right place for you, even though you've gotten what appears to be an

attractive job offer. The more informed and careful you are before signing on, the better positioned you should be to deal with inevitable setbacks.

Special Considerations for Real Estate Decisions

Real estate investment decisions are undoubtedly the toughest ones to make. With all those digits in the sticker price, buying a home is rightfully frightening. But it's not only about all that money; it's also about the actual and implied commitment to establish roots and stay put for a while. Selling a home is no picnic either, especially since most people buy another home after selling. That's two transactions—double the stress and the headaches.

Given the ever-present economic worries and other issues in life we face, along with all the associated uncertainty, people often ask me if they should buy a house instead of renting or if they should sell their home. My short answer is that it depends on your local real estate market and your personal situation. One of my favorite analyses to determine whether buying or renting is advisable is to compare the monthly cost of renting a given home to the monthly (after-tax) cost of owning that same home (mortgage payment + property taxes + insurance + maintenance – tax benefits). You shouldn't be paying a large premium to buy and own. If the ownership costs greatly exceed the rental costs, renting is a better value and ultimately may attract enough prospective buyers to weaken housing prices.

If you're a renter who has been thinking about buying, you're in a market that's already weak, and you're motivated to buy, you can probably get a decent deal on purchasing a home, especially if the rental costs of a given property are close to the ownership costs. That's not to say that prices won't fall further after your purchase. But you should accept the fact that none of us has a crystal ball and realize that once it's clear that times are getting better, the market will likely have moved higher.

If your local real estate market is just beginning to show signs of weakness, renting is a good value, and you have some personal ambivalence about buying, you should probably wait. Perhaps your job is at risk due to your employer's financial situation or the industry you're in. Maybe you don't wish to stay in your current geographic area for much longer.

Purchasing and then ultimately selling a home is a costly proposition. You've got loan fees, real estate agent commissions, title costs, and other expenses that can easily gobble up 15 percent of the home's value between the two transactions. That's why I suggest that you plan to hold on to your home for at least three and preferably five years. Expecting 15 percent appreciation just to cover your transaction costs over shorter time frames is foolish.

With regards to selling, if you must sell because you have to move, price your house realistically. If a locally softening economy gets you depressed because your house doesn't net as much as you expected, remember that when you buy, you'll benefit from the lower prices unless you're "unlucky" to be moving from a depressed housing market into a strong one.

Don't consider opportunistic selling—selling now and expecting to buy back in after a big price drop. Real estate prices don't plunge in a recession. It's also impossible to call the bottom. And remember all those transaction costs. Over the decades of your adult life, owning a home should be a wise investment. You've just got to accept some down periods along the way. The fact that you can't easily trade or sell a house for little cost is actually a good thing. Unlike the ease of selling stocks, homeowners tend to hold on for longer periods of time and profit because of the longer-term appreciation of the housing market.

THE OBSESSIVE: GAMBLING AND OTHER ADDICTIVE BEHAVIORS

Carl installed new software on his office computer that allows him to follow his stock portfolio minute by minute. This enables him to constantly monitor his stocks during the trading day, and when a supervisor or someone else is nearby whom he doesn't want to see what he's doing, he simply minimizes that part of his computer screen. When Carl is away on vacation, he carries a PDA (a personal digital assistant) with him so he can receive stock price updates and alerts. After promising his family that their vacation would be "work" free, he constantly invents scenarios to steal away and check the stock ticker. He lies to them at the hotel pool, for example, claiming that he needs to go back to the room to get his sunglasses when he simply wants to check on his stocks' prices. Carl has major control issues with his investments that he has learned correspond with his drinking problems.

Carl is far from unusual. Today, more Americans than ever have trouble breaking free of one or more addictions. The financial, physical, mental, personal, and spiritual costs of gambling, smoking, drinking excessively, abusing other substances, and overeating are staggering. The majority of premature deaths and health-care dollars spent on medical conditions are caused by these addictions.

Addictive behaviors undermine sound personal financial management. Most addictions are costly, especially when viewed in terms of what that money could've done for you had you invested it rather than squandering it gambling, drinking, smoking, or on some other habit. Cigarettes, alcohol, and drugs are expensive. And you can blow through significant dough in short order gambling. (I'll quantify the financial costs, along with many others, of various addictions later in this chapter.)

Having worked at giving financial advice for well over a decade, I can honestly say that addictions are the primary impediment to accomplishing money goals. People with addictions have great difficulty changing their behaviors and habits. This chapter highlights problems with gambling, drinking, smoking, and substance abuse. Plus, the ability to quickly and easily trade investments, especially through the Internet, has created a whole new set of problematic, addictive behavior. All of these issues have associated costs and are closely aligned with common financial problems. Having identified common addictions, I will then discuss the keys to breaking costly and destructive addictions and the treatment programs that work.

America the Addicted

This chapter isn't the first in the book to discuss addictions. Portions of Chapters 2 and 3, for example, are devoted to addictions—to shopping and spending and to work. This chapter covers other major addictions that have touched virtually every family, including:

Gambling. Unbelievably, the (legalized) gambling industry, euphemistically called the gaming business, now rakes in more than $80 billion annually, which is greater than the amount that Americans spend on tickets to sporting events, movies, theme parks, plays, concerts and live performances, and music combined!

Drugs. Addiction to illegal and legal drugs is a massive problem in the United States. Various studies estimate that upwards of 20 million people currently use illegal drugs. Millions more wrestle with addiction problems involving tranquilizers, stimulants, and the nonmedical use of various prescription painkillers, such as Vicodin, Percodan, Lorcet, Hydrocodone, and OxyContin. If these latter three sound familiar, it may be because of radio talk-show titan Rush Limbaugh's public fall after authorities caught him having people illegally buying these drugs to feed his addiction.

Alcohol. Although the numbers of Americans abusing drugs are staggering in their own right, alcohol abuse is an even bigger problem. More than 50 million Americans are classified as binge drinkers (imbibing five or more drinks at a single occasion at least once per month). Nearly 20 million of these people can be considered chronic heavy drinkers, as they have at least five drinking binges monthly.

Smoking. More than 70 million Americans engage in this costly and life-threatening habit. Approximately half a million Americans die each year due to smoking, which makes it the number-one preventable cause of death in the United States. The indictments against smoking are staggering, but just consider a few more statistics: 20 percent of all heart-disease fatalities, 30 percent of all cancer deaths, and 25 percent of all residential fire casualties are attributable to smoking.

FOOD ADDICTIONS: MORE DAMAGING TO HEALTH THAN WALLET

Obesity and food addictions are interrelated and on the rise among not only adults but also our children. Approximately two-thirds of Americans are now considered overweight, and about one in three is obese. Poor eating habits combined with other lifestyle problems, such as a lack of exercise, are contributing to high rates of heart disease, cancer, and diabetes, and ultimately to higher health-care costs.

Studies by the American Cancer Society have found that the risks of contracting various deadly cancers due to obesity are now on par with those associated with smoking. Obesity-related conditions are killing almost as many Americans annually as smoking and may soon surpass smoking as the number-one cause of preventable deaths.

Most food addictions cause people to eat lower-quality, relatively inexpensive, and highly processed foods. Thus, unlike the other addictions discussed in this chapter, food addictions don't generally "cost" people financially. Although, in the long run, such unhealthy dietary habits lead to greater health-care expenditures, most people find that to eat healthier, they spend as much or more on food.

Gambling with Your Future

Legalized gambling got off to a slow start in the twentieth century. The first casino opened in Nevada in 1931, and it wasn't until forty-five years later, in 1976, that the first casino opened in another state, this time in Atlantic City, New Jersey. Today, more than 1,300 casinos operate in thirty-six states. Members of about one-third of American households visit a casino annually, and they average approximately six casino trips per year. Even closer to home, and much more accessible, are state and multi-state lotteries. New Hampshire was the first state to have a lottery, but today more than three-quarters of states run lotteries. Add in horse racing, dog racing, off-track betting, jai alai, Internet gambling, and video poker machines, and you quickly realize that Americans have a mushrooming number of opportunities to gamble away their money. In fact, forty-eight states now offer some form of legalized gambling (only Hawaii and Utah are left free of gaming).

Not surprisingly, accompanying this surge in available gambling options is an increase in the percentage of Americans with a serious gambling problem, a fact confirmed by studies by the Harvard Medical School Division on Addictions; Marc Potenza, director of Yale's Problem Gambling Clinic; and good old-fashioned common sense. Also consider that the introduction of a major gambling establishment approximately doubles the number of problem gamblers within a fifty-mile radius, according to an analysis done by the National Opinion Research Center. For so-called problem gamblers, gambling interferes with work, family life, friendships, and personal money management.

Casinos know the extent of the problem, and they take steps to exploit it. They're well known for developing and utilizing mailing lists targeting compulsive gamblers—their best customers. These establishments inundate their biggest spending customers with an avalanche of solicitations inviting these profligate gamblers to make free use of their hotel rooms, check out a sporting event on the house, and attend private cocktail parties, among other amenities. Who better to drop a lot of dough in the casino than a tipsy, addicted gambler?

In the end, that's what problem gamblers do—they drop a lot of dough. Then, they typically rack up more debt to feed their money-losing ways by borrowing on credit cards, through casino credit lines, and from acquaintances until they ultimately end up in bankruptcy. In a study published in the *American Journal of Psychiatry,* a whopping 85 percent of callers to a problem-gambling help line reported financial problems due to their gambling. However, the financial strains induced by gambling are only one component of the problem.

Problem gamblers are four times more likely to abuse alcohol than the average person, more than eight times more likely to struggle with drug-abuse issues, and have a much greater incidence of divorce, child abuse, and domestic violence within the family. Gamblers also suffer from extremely high rates of psychological problems: 90 percent experience high rates of anxiety, and 80 percent suffer from depression caused by their gambling. These rates are nearly the same as those attributed to cocaine use by callers to a cocaine help line.

Dr. Hans Breiter, a psychiatry professor at Harvard Medical School, has published research documenting that both gambling and cocaine stimulate the same region of the brain that produces dopamine. "We cannot distinguish any difference between the brain pattern of someone gambling and someone ingesting cocaine," says Breiter.

As I mentioned earlier, our own governments are also contributing to the problem, through state-sanctioned lotteries. Some people have been duped into believing that state lotteries are actually useful. The argument is that they supposedly help lower taxes and fund education, but states actually take in little revenue from lotteries—only about one-third of the money generated through ticket sales (the rest goes to prizes and administration). That percentage compares quite unfavorably with the track record of charities, which are able to deliver about 80 percent of the money they bring in to the actual cause. Numerous analyses that I've seen clearly demonstrate that states with lotteries have higher, not lower, taxes and spend less on education than states without lotteries. But lotteries are viewed by many lawmakers and constituents as "free" money. State governments are addicted to gambling revenue, especially when they're running deficits. Unlike cutting spending or increasing taxes, few people are motivated and mobilized to protest state promotion of gambling, as the true costs are often hidden within individual families.

Substance Abusers' Families Shoulder the Burdens

To the outside world, Rachel was an intelligent, warm, caring mother of two who lived in a beautiful home in California with her husband, Bruce, to whom outsiders would have attributed the same qualities. Inside their home, however, Rachel struggled to keep her family together despite Bruce's drinking problems and their repeated marital separations.

Although an affair that Bruce had caused the initial separation, over the years it was Bruce's addiction to alcohol that ultimately destroyed his marriage, caused his death at the age of

A PSYCHOLOGIST AND CHILD DEVELOPMENT EXPERT'S TAKE ON GAMBLING, BY DR. JAMES DOBSON

Focus on the Family opposes all forms of legalized gambling for both moral and pragmatic reasons. We believe the net societal effect of our government's embrace of gambling has been disastrous.

Gambling is driven by and subsists on greed. For this reason, the activity is morally bankrupt from its very foundation. Gambling is also an activity that exploits the vulnerable—the young, the old, and those susceptible to addictive behaviors. Further, gambling entices the financially disadvantaged classes with the unrealistic hope of escape from poverty through instant riches, thus ultimately worsening the plight of our poorest citizens. Also, gambling undermines the work ethic. It is based on the premise of something for nothing, a concept that sanctions idleness rather than industriousness, slothfulness instead of initiative.

The more tangible downsides to gambling are similarly disturbing. Legalized gambling breeds a host of social ills, as has been demonstrated time and time again in areas where gambling has been introduced on a widespread basis.

Legalized gambling creates gambling addicts. An abundance of research and expert testimony demonstrates that as gambling expands, so does the number of those with serious gambling problems. Millions more Americans have developed devastating gambling addictions over the last few years as a direct result of gambling's rapid proliferation. Further, these newly created addicts are the lifeblood of the industry. Preliminary research indicates that a third or more of gambling revenues come from problem and pathological gamblers.

Gambling breeds crime. Communities that welcome gambling also welcome an increase in crime. Recent history in communities ranging from Atlantic City to Deadwood, South Dakota, to the Mississippi Gulf Coast indicates that the sheer number of crimes skyrockets in an area once gambling is permitted. Much of this is attributed to the newly created gambling addicts who, in desperation, turn to crime to finance their addiction. Also, legalized gambling makes an attractive target for career criminals. Organized crime has infiltrated numerous legal gambling operations in various states in recent years.

Gambling is an economic negative. Many states and communities embrace gambling as a means to generate additional revenues as well as to inspire economic growth, boost tourism, and create jobs. Gambling's ability to do all of these is either greatly exaggerated or nonexistent. For instance, gambling often hurts, not helps, existing businesses by siphoning away discretionary dollars that might otherwise have been spent at local shops. Also, the social costs associated with gambling—such as losses due to crime, additional law enforcement costs, gambling addiction treatment costs, and lost work productivity—are staggering, often far exceeding a state or community's total revenues from gambling.

Legalized gambling devastates families. Authorities in gambling jurisdictions report dramatic increases in divorce, suicide, bankruptcy, and child abuse and domestic violence related to gambling. Research shows that children of gambling addicts experience lower levels of mental health and physical well-being.

Given these and other considerations, it is unconscionable that our government would continue to allow—and even promote—gambling activities. Legalized gambling is ravaging the lives of untold thousands of individuals and families, and contributes substantially to the moral decay of our communities. Therefore, we believe legalized gambling, in all its forms, should and must be vigorously opposed.

Dr. Dobson is founder and chairman of Focus on the Family. Copyright, Focus on the Family and http://www.family.org. Reprinted with permission.

forty-eight, and wreaked havoc with the family's finances. "After the final separation and subsequent divorce, Bruce wasn't attending to his business, which required a lot of customer service. . . . When he died, I lost my alimony and child support," says Rachel, adding, "95 percent of my financial difficulties were due to the alcoholism."

Because alcoholics are so adept at concealing their problems and family members and friends often aren't able to pinpoint the problem or overcome their denial, the disease of alcoholism can go on for many years, often until it's too late to save the alcoholic. Substance abusers of all types ultimately cause enormous damage to their households' finances and often don't get the help they need until those around them understand the problem and how to deal with it.

Alcoholism and substance-abuse problems, which often go hand in hand, are widespread and costly to both individual families and society as a whole. "When the effects on the families of abusers and people close to those injured or killed by intoxicated drivers are considered, such abuse affects untold millions more," says the American Psychiatric Association. More than 41 percent of the nation's 42,000 annual traffic fatalities and more than 1 million injuries occur annually in alcohol-related traffic crashes according to the National Highway Traffic Safety Administration. Approximately two in every five Americans will be involved in an alcohol-related crash at some time in their lives, and over each decade, four times as many Americans die in drunk-driving crashes as were killed in the Vietnam War. Traffic crashes, about half of which are alcohol related, are the single greatest cause of death for everyone between the ages of five and twenty-seven. The American Medical Association estimates that about one-third of the patients occupying general hospital beds are under treatment for ailments resulting from alcoholism.

As a society, we have a warped perception of who alcoholics are. Many of us think of the visible alcoholics and drug abusers whom we see wandering the streets. "Only about 3 percent of alcoholics are the problem on the street. . . . [T]he other 97 percent cuts across the population," says Michael Webb, a mental health professional who works with companies through employee assistance programs. Alcoholism, which often goes hand in hand with drug abuse, has brought many famous people into treatment. The list includes former first lady Betty Ford; Kitty Dukakis, wife of presidential candidate Michael Dukakis; former NBA basketball player Chris Mullin; and Mary Tyler Moore and has led to the early death of others, including William Holden, Mickey Mantle, Elvis Presley, and comedian Chris Farley. However, most alcoholics and substance abusers aren't famous from their work, nor are they down-and-out street people. To the rest of us, they appear to be ordinary people with strengths and weaknesses. In fact, like Bruce, alcoholics can be great employees, well educated, have top-paying professional jobs, and provide for their families for a long time. Family members, however, see more of the dark side. According to Rachel, "Bruce entertained clients and drank, and [he] also drank with other family members. . . . He often didn't come home until late and became belligerent and argumentative. Everyone on the outside thought we had it made. We had a nice home, he drove a Mercedes, and we had two healthy kids. But Bruce was so unhappy."

Bruce was successful and making money, but he wasn't good at managing it. He didn't come from a financially stable home, and he loved having a lot of money in his pocket and spending it. "He was reckless with his money and liked to spend it on status items to show the world he had arrived and fit into the mold of his peers. He was terrible at saving money and spent a lot on alcohol and eating out," says Rachel.

Problems dealing with money can be an indicator of possible substance-abuse problems and provide a clue to family, friends, and counselors that further investigation is necessary. Financial signs can include those that seem to result from carelessness but become chronic, such as late or unpaid bills, overdrawn checking accounts, maxing out sources of credit, and neglecting to tell a spouse or partner about purchases. Gambling problems and workplace difficulties often correlate with chemical addiction. "In the workplace, other possible indicators of such addictions include wage garnishments for debts, problems with expense accounts such as getting way behind in reports or paying back cash advances, and a bankruptcy filing," adds Webb.

Even with financial warning flags and other concerns, such as drunk-driving incidents, frequent arguments in the home, and accompanying medical ailments that often come with substance abuse, even immediate family members often can't identify the exact problem (or they're in denial about it). Rachel illustrates this challenge: "Bruce was really good at keeping his addiction a secret . . . but it got harder over time as he started drinking in the morning. Part of me was in denial. It wasn't until one of Bruce's office assistants said that she thought he was an alcoholic did I really begin to consider the possibility. I was an enabler. Bruce had always been attracted to people who could take care of him and cover for him."

In psychology circles, enablers like Rachel are referred to as "codependents." In an interview aired on the CBS News program *60 Minutes,* former president Gerald Ford admitted to his own codependent behavior that created an accepting environment for his wife Betty's drinking: "I was a bad enabler. I made all kinds of excuses, made all kinds of alibis [for Betty]. That's a typical spouse's reaction." As is often the case, according to psychologists and substance-abuse experts, the reach of codependency extends to children of alcoholics, as well as spouses, and sometimes to friends and coworkers. Betty Ford's adult children, for example, used to water down her drinks at functions where alcohol was served.

Betty Ford finally got the help she needed when confronted by family members in a formal intervention. "They went from one to another saying how I had let them down, how I disappointed them. . . . I was so hurt. I felt I had spent my whole life devoted to them, and they were telling me I was failing them," she said about the intervention. This tough-love approach worked with her. "The intervention was the only thing that saved Betty's life," claimed Gerald Ford in the *60 Minutes* interview. Within a week of the intervention, Betty Ford entered and successfully completed an inpatient alcohol-treatment program at the Long Beach Naval Hospital's Alcohol and Drug Rehabilitation Unit and has been sober since. In fact, she has been a champion of alcohol treatment. She founded and has maintained an active involvement in the Betty Ford Treatment Center, which has been in operation since 1982 and has treated more than 60,000 patients.

The alcoholic not only needs to quit drinking but also needs to address the underlying psychological issues accompanying the behavior. Those close to the alcoholic should also address such issues, as they're at high risk (especially children of alcoholics) for becoming alcoholics themselves. "People who come to me because a spouse or a child has a drinking problem often are reluctant to go into psychological counseling—some really hate looking at themselves," says Webb. Recovered alcoholics will tell you that doing so is difficult but well worth the effort.

Smoking: A Costly and Deadly Habit

Despite the clear and urgent health warnings about smoking that have been sounded for more than four decades, three in ten adults still smoke. The 1964 *Surgeon General's Report on Smoking and Health,* prepared under Dr. Luther L. Terry, was the first compilation of the ills caused by tobacco usage. Thanks to this report and thousands of subsequent medical studies, there's irrefutable proof of how and why a half million Americans die annually from smoking. Tobacco contains countless poisonous chemicals including the highly addictive nicotine, carbon monoxide, ammonia, aldehydes, and tars. The regular inhalation of this toxic brew causes heart disease, stroke, emphysema (and other chronic obstructive pulmonary diseases), lung cancer, and numerous other cancers including those of the esophagus, mouth, kidney, and bladder. So-called secondhand smoke has also been proven to cause heart and respiratory problems, including lung cancer, in spouses and others frequently around smokers.

As people die due to continued usage, the tobacco industry must, of course, recruit its next generation of customers and victims. Smoking campaigns are targeted at young adults, with great success: Four in ten adults between the ages of eighteen and twenty-five smoke. In addition, one in eight kids between the ages of twelve and seventeen smokes despite the fact that it's illegal for minors to buy tobacco.

Smokers know that, at $4 per pack, cigarette smoking is expensive. But let me crunch some numbers for you and provide a new financial perspective. Take a smoker who goes through just one pack per day. In addition to the health damage, consider the opportunity cost of having spent that money on smoking rather than investing it. If you took that $4 per day and invested in a diversified portfolio of stocks in a tax-advantaged retirement account, over twenty years, you'd have about $128,000, and in forty years, you'd have amassed approximately $1 million. At just one pack per day, cigarette smoking is a million-dollar habit! Those who smoke more than one pack a day have a multimillion-dollar habit.

Overcoming Addictions

Millions of people have successfully conquered costly and deadly addictions. Doing so isn't easy or quick. "Addiction is a chronic disease, like diabetes, asthma, or hypertension. Just like these diseases, one course of treatment is unlikely to result in a complete cure. Ongoing treatment may be required before an addict achieves the final stage of recovery," says the Institute for Research, Education, and Training in Addictions.

Consider the following hurdles standing in the way of individuals with addictions getting the treatment that they need:

Denial.   Many people with addictions aren't willing or able to admit their problem and the damage it's causing to themselves and their loved ones. Others may understand some of the problems, but they aren't ready to give up their coveted substances and behaviors.

Shame.   The enormous humiliation that many people who suffer addictions feel often prevents them from seeking help. To help substance-abuse sufferers combat these feelings, many twelve-step programs, such as Alcoholics Anonymous, provide a high level of confidentiality.

Uncertainty surrounding their options.   Even when people are motivated to finally get help, sorting through all the treatment options and determining which ones may work best for them can be time consuming and intimidating. A general lack of knowledge about and a reluctance to offer unsolicited referrals for substance-abuse treatment on the part of many primary care physicians exacerbate this problem. When presented with an adult patient with the early symptoms of alcohol abuse, a whopping 94 percent of primary care doctors failed to include substance abuse among the five possible diagnoses that they offered. This disturbing finding comes from a survey conducted by the National Center on Addiction and Substance Abuse (CASA) at Columbia University. Among the reasons, according to the report, that physicians are missing or misdiagnosing patients' substance abuse are lack of adequate medical school training, skepticism about treatment effectiveness, patient resistance, discomfort discussing substance abuse, time constraints, and fear of losing patients.

Cost. I've discussed how costly many addictions are, but the cost of treatment is perceived to be much higher because its cost is incurred over short periods of time. Insurance, unfortunately, often doesn't cover many treatments. "The best treatment programs for you depend upon how much money you have. Insurance won't generally pay for 28-day inpatient-stay programs," says Dr. John Morgenstern, vice president of health and treatment at CASA. Plus, consumers who understand the insurance business are justifiably worried that disclosing an addiction like alcoholism or other substance abuse will be a black mark against them in terms of future insurance availability and cost. Before ruling out any treatment options, though, be sure that you understand the range of alternatives, the costs associated with each, and the portion of those costs that your health insurance will pay.

Time constraints. Even if someone locates good treatment options and determines how to pay for the needed help, carving out the necessary time is another not-so-insignificant hurdle. Treatment is time consuming, and work and family demands can stand in the way. Most employees don't wish to disclose their problem or treatment plans to their bosses and coworkers because few employers foster an environment in which employees can feel secure in disclosing their treatment needs.

Gambling Treatment Options

In 1979, the American Psychiatric Association recognized gambling as a disease. Numerous insurers now cover some therapy

and treatment for people with gambling problems. The preva-
lence of associated mental health problems in gamblers clearly
shows that gamblers need to be treated with appropriate mental health services. Some gamblers have found success in conquering their addiction by enlisting the support of spouses,
partners, or friends and turning the family finances over to their
spouses. If you or someone you love has a need for gambling-
related treatment programs and resources, consider the following resources.

The Web site of the National Council on Problem Gambling
has an excellent resource section (http://www.ncpgambling.
org/resources) that contains a compendium of online and
print resources for gamblers seeking help and a directory of
treatment programs and counselors. Here, you will also find a
useful list of issues to consider and questions to ask when evaluating various treatment programs. The organization also offers
a 24/7 help line at 1-800-522-4700, through which you can obtain a confidential referral to a counselor.

Gamblers Anonymous (http://www.gamblersanonymous.
org; 1-213-386-8789) is a twelve-step organization that began in
1957. The organization's Web site details the twelve-step approach to conquering a gambling addiction and lists meeting
locations organized by country (and by state within the United
States). The sister organization, Gam-Anon, also offers a useful
Web site (http://www.gam-anon.org) tailored to the needs
and concerns of family and friends of those suffering from a
gambling addiction.

The more comprehensive treatment centers, such as the
Hazelden Foundation and Sierra Tucson, discussed in the
next section, handle gambling problems and associated mental disorders.

GAMBLERS ANONYMOUS TWENTY QUESTIONS FOR DETERMINING COMPULSIVE GAMBLING

Earlier, I describe many of the effects gambling can have on individuals and families. And though you need to contact experts in the matter using the resources I provide here, you can use this self-diagnostic test to see if you may have a compulsive gambling problem. According to Gamblers Anonymous, a person who has a compulsive gambling problem will answer yes to seven or more of these twenty questions.

1. Did you ever lose time from work or school due to gambling?
2. Has gambling ever made your home life unhappy?
3. Did gambling affect your reputation?
4. Have you ever felt remorse after gambling?
5. Did you ever gamble to get money with which to pay debts or otherwise solve financial difficulties?
6. Did gambling cause a decrease in your ambition or efficiency?
7. After losing, did you feel you must return as soon as possible and win back your losses?
8. After a win did you have a strong urge to return and win more?
9. Did you often gamble until your last dollar was gone?
10. Did you ever borrow to finance your gambling?
11. Have you ever sold anything to finance gambling?
12. Were you reluctant to use "gambling money" for normal expenditures?

13. Did gambling make you careless of the welfare of yourself or your family?
14. Did you ever gamble longer than you had planned?
15. Have you ever gambled to escape worry or trouble?
16. Have you ever committed, or considered committing, an illegal act to finance gambling?
17. Did gambling cause you to have difficulty in sleeping?
18. Do arguments, disappointments, or frustrations create within you an urge to gamble?
19. Did you ever have an urge to celebrate any good fortune by a few hours of gambling?
20. Have you ever considered self destruction or suicide as a result of your gambling?

Alcoholism and Drug Treatment Resources

A simple yet powerful diagnostic tool used within the medical community for screening for alcoholism is the CAGE questionnaire, which was originally discussed by Allen, Eckardt, and Wallen in the journal *Public Health Reports* in 1988. CAGE is composed of just four questions:

Have you felt the need to **C**ut down on your drinking?
Do you feel **A**nnoyed by people complaining about your drinking?
Do you ever feel **G**uilty about your drinking?
Do you ever drink an **E**ye-opener in the morning to relieve the shakes?

The study found that those individuals who are "problem drinkers" will answer at least two of these questions yes.

Alcoholics Anonymous, a treatment program discussed later in this section, has twelve questions that you can also ask yourself (note the similarities with some of the CAGE questions):

1. Have you ever decided to stop drinking for a week or so but lasted for only a couple of days?
2. Do you wish people would mind their own business about your drinking—stop telling you what to do?
3. Have you ever switched from one kind of drink to another in the hope that this would keep you from getting drunk?
4. Have you had to have an eye-opener upon awakening during the past year?
5. Do you envy people who can drink without getting into trouble?
6. Have you had problems connected with drinking during the past year?
7. Has your drinking caused trouble at home?
8. Do you ever try to get "extra" drinks at a party because you do not get enough?
9. Do you tell yourself you can stop drinking any time you want to, even though you keep getting drunk when you don't mean to?
10. Have you missed days of work or school because of drinking?
11. Do you have "blackouts"?
12. Have you ever felt that your life would be better if you did not drink?

Alcoholics Anonymous says that if you answered yes at least four times, you are likely in trouble with your alcohol use.

Among the best resources for alcoholics and those who care about them are the following:

- The National Council on Alcoholism and Drug Dependence (http://www.ncadd.org; 1-212-269-7797). This nonprofit, which seeks to educate and advocate prevention, intervention, and treatment through its national affiliate network, was founded in 1944 by Marty Mann, the first female "graduate" of Alcoholics Anonymous.
- The U.S. Department of Health and Human Services Substance Abuse and Mental Health Services Administration Web site (http://www.samhsa.gov) offers a user-friendly substance abuse treatment facility locator, or you can call their referral help line at 1-800-662-4357.
- Alcoholics Anonymous (http://www.aa.org; 1-212-870-3400) is a self-help twelve-step group program for alcoholics. Al-Anon (http://www.alanon.org; 1-888-425-2666) is a self-help twelve-step group program for friends and family of alcoholics. The Web sites of both organizations can provide you with local contact information (or check your phone directory for nearby chapters).
- The Boston University School of Public Health offers a Web site (http://www.alcoholscreening.org) that includes educational materials, a searchable database of treatment resources, and links to various support groups.
- The Betty Ford Center (http://www.bettyfordcenter.org; 1-800-854-9211) is a nonprofit alcohol and drug treatment program

cofounded by former first lady Betty Ford after her own successful alcohol treatment. The center offers inpatient services for both those suffering from addictions and their family members.

- The Hazelden Foundation (http://www.hazelden.org; 1-800-257-7810) offers treatment programs in Minnesota, Oregon, Illinois, and New York. Hazelden takes patient education seriously, as is evidenced by the extensive list of quality publications that the organization produces and sells. Its Web site also contains much free information.
- The Caron Foundation (http://www.caron.org; 1-800-678-2332) is a Pennsylvania-based nonprofit drug and alcohol treatment program that also has centers in New York and Florida.
- Columbia Presbyterian (1-212-305-6001) offers a couple of different treatment venues—McKeen and the Retreat—that are known for handling the more complex cases of substance abuse that also involve medical and psychiatric problems.
- Sierra Tucson (http://www.sierratucson.com; 1-800-842-4487) provides inpatient treatment for a variety of problems, including substance abuse, gambling, eating disorders, and associated mental health issues.

Smoking-Cessation Programs

In recent years, public education has made some progress in getting Americans to light up less and quit altogether. However, change has been relatively slow, and far too many people still smoke way too much. The following are among the more

SOME PRACTICAL ADVICE FROM AN EMERGENCY ROOM PHYSICIAN

Just after Princess Diana died in a grisly auto accident, various magazines and newspapers devoted entire issues and special sections to her life and tragic death. Amid all of this coverage, I found some wonderful pearls of wisdom from Dr. Thomas Meadoff, who wrote an editorial in the *San Francisco Chronicle*. Meadoff stated that he was on duty in an emergency room when he first heard about Princess Diana's death. The news media at the time were focusing on the paparazzi doggedly pursuing Diana's speeding car that night in an attempt to get yet another picture or story about her love life and other personal details.

> I thought, at the time, the lessons were immediately apparent without further details. And they had nothing to do with paparazzi. As someone who publicly crusaded against devices and diseases, which maim and kill children and adults in the prime of life, Diana may have wanted these lessons to have received more emphasis than the misdirected press coverage so far:
>
> 1. Don't drink and drive.
> 2. Don't get in the car with a driver who has been drinking.
> 3. Wear your seat belt.
> 4. Don't speed.
>
> Allowing for the occasional exception, if there is an auto accident with a severe injury, a seat belt wasn't worn. At 120 mph, any vehicle, even a lead-plated Mercedes, is a murder weapon. You can do it all by yourself, without the paparazzi. Do yourself and your family a favor. I don't need the business.

Well said!

INTERVENTIONS

Getting addicted people into needed treatment is often difficult and may feel impossible given all of the obstacles discussed earlier in this chapter—time, costs, shame, denial, and not knowing where to turn for help. Interventions can help overcome these problems.

In a typical intervention, a paid professional (the interventionist) brings together family and friends to "confront" the person with the addiction. This is how Betty Ford's family got her into alcohol treatment. Relatives often turn to an intervention when they've exhausted other avenues for help or don't know how to proceed. To learn more about interventions, please consult the following books: *Intervention: How to Help Someone Who Doesn't Want Help* by Vernon E. Johnson (Hazelden), *Love First: A New Approach to Intervention for Alcoholism and Drug Addiction* by Jeff Jay and Debra Jay (Hazelden), and *The Betty Ford Center Book of Answers* by James W. West (Pocket Books).

useful smoking-cessation resources and programs. When compared to seeking help for alcohol and drug addictions, your search for smoking-cessation programs will yield many lower-cost alternatives.

- The U.S. Public Health Service convened a panel of smoking-cessation experts to compile a summary of treatment protocols that have proven effective.

Although the document you will find at http://
www.surgeongeneral.gov/tobacco/tobaqrg.htm is
targeted to physicians, it contains a treasure trove of
useful information on quitting smoking.

- QuitNet grew out of research done at the Boston
University School of Public Health and now operates
as a private company, partly owned by the university.
To access the Web site (http://www.quitnet.com), you
must register. One of the basic premises of the site is
that social support is important to stopping smoking.
Basic services, such as a guide to quitting smoking and
access to support forums, are free. The premium
membership, which costs forty dollars for three
months and one hundred dollars for one year,
includes one-on-one counseling, online group
counseling, additional printed materials featuring
expert advice, medication advice, and discounts on
smoking-cessation medication.

- Nicotine Anonymous (http://www.nicotine-
anonymous.org; 1-415-750-0328) is another twelve-
step program, albeit with fewer meeting locations
than the other twelve-step programs recommended in
this chapter.

- The Hazelden Foundation (http://www.hazelden.org;
1-800-257-7800) offers an inpatient smoking-cessation
program in Minnesota.

- The Champaign-Urbana (Illinois) Public Health
District has two excellent booklets to convince and
help you to quit smoking. Visit http://www.mckinley.
uiuc.edu/Wellness/AlcoholandDrugs/stepbystep/
stepbystep.htm.

MOTIVATION TO QUIT SMOKING

Within 20 minutes after you smoke that last cigarette, your body begins a series of changes that continue for years.

20 minutes after quitting: Your heart rate drops.

12 hours after quitting: Carbon monoxide levels in your blood drops to normal.

2 weeks to 3 months after quitting: Your heart attack risk begins to drop. Your lung function begins to improve.

1 to 9 months after quitting: Your coughing and shortness of breath decrease.

1 year after quitting: Your added risk of coronary heart disease is half that of a smoker's.

5 to 15 years after quitting: Your stroke risk is reduced to that of a nonsmoker's.

10 years after quitting: Your lung cancer death rate is about half that of a smoker's. Your risk of cancers of the mouth, throat, esophagus, bladder, kidney, and pancreas decreases.

15 years after quitting: Your risk of coronary heart disease is back to that of a nonsmoker's.

U.S. Department for Health and Human Services,
Centers for Disease Control and Prevention.

Protecting Teens and Kids

Companies and individuals who profit from addictions are always seeking new recruits. The best strategy to attract and retain long-term customers is to target teenagers (and in some cases younger kids), who are the easiest converts due to their susceptibility to peer-group pressure and undeveloped decision-making skills. Parents must protect their children who are so vulnerable and easily swayed to take risky and dangerous actions. Consider these statistics: the average age of first-time alcohol use is twelve years and two months, followed by twelve years and six months for cigarettes and thirteen years and eleven months for marijuana (the most popular illegal drug among adolescents).

How high are the stakes? "A child who reaches age 21 without smoking, abusing alcohol or using drugs is virtually certain never to do so," says Joseph A. Califano Jr., chairman and president of the National Center on Addiction and Substance Abuse at Columbia University and a former secretary of the U.S. Department of Health, Education, and Welfare.

The risk that teens will smoke, drink, get drunk, and use illegal drugs increases sharply if they are highly stressed, frequently bored, or have substantial amounts of spending money, according to the *National Survey of American Attitudes on Substance Abuse VIII: Teens and Parents,* a survey conducted by CASA. Among CASA's survey findings:

- High-stress teens are twice as likely as low-stress teens to smoke, drink, get drunk, and use illegal drugs.
- Often-bored teens are 50 percent likelier than not-often-bored teens to smoke, drink, get drunk, and use illegal drugs.
- Teens with twenty-five dollars or more a week in spending money are nearly twice as likely as teens with less to smoke, drink, and use illegal drugs and more than twice as likely to get drunk.

- Teens exhibiting two or three of these characteristics
  are at more than three times the risk of substance
  abuse as those exhibiting none of these characteristics.

"High stress, frequent boredom and too much spending money are a catastrophic combination for many American teens," said Califano. "But it is a catastrophe that can be avoided through parental engagement. Parents must be sensitive to the stress in their children's lives, understand why they are bored and limit their spending money."

The CASA survey also found that parents are more likely than teens to view teen drug use as a fait accompli. More than four out of ten parents said teens are "very likely" or "somewhat likely" to try drugs, compared to only one of ten teens who agreed with those statements. Teens whose parents believe that future drug use is "very likely" are more than three times more likely to become substance abusers than teens whose parents say future drug use is "not likely at all." More than half of parents whose children attend schools where drugs are used, kept, or sold wouldn't send their teen to a drug-free school if they could. Asked why, these parents answered: no schools are drug free (54 percent), kids should make their own choices (22 percent), drugs are not a problem (11 percent), and the child likes his or her school (7 percent). "Many parents think they have little power over their teens' substance use and a disturbing number view drugs in schools as a fact of life they are powerless to stop," noted Califano. "How parents act, how much pressure they put on school administrators to get drugs out of their teens' schools, their attitudes about drugs, and how engaged they are in their children's lives will have enormous influence over their teens' substance use. Parent Power is the most underutilized weapon in efforts to curb teen substance abuse."

CASA recommended five ways that parents can reduce the risk of their teens engaging in smoking, drinking, or other substance abuse:

Be sensitive to the stress in your children's lives and help them cope. Kids today face all sorts of peer pressure in school to fit in socially. Academic pressures are problematic as well, particularly in high school and when children are preparing to apply to colleges. I can tell you as an alumni interviewer for my alma mater (Yale) that many of the kids I speak with today are leading the lives of overscheduled little adults. A twelve-hour day isn't unusual for high school kids: after a seven-hour school day, most of these kids spend several hours on extracurricular activities and several more on homework.

Understand when and why your children are bored and help relieve their boredom. Children don't need nonstop entertainment, and you certainly won't be doing the best by your kids if you constantly plan out their days, activities, and social calendar. However, at key times, you can play a vital role in helping them to recognize opportunities and keep them from likely trouble.

Limit the amount of money your children have to spend and monitor how that money is spent. A simple way to track kids' spending is to have them use a VISA or MasterCard debit card that limits what they can spend because it's connected to a checking account that you monitor.

Know who your children's friends are. Spend time speaking with their parents. Never assume—ask questions.

Be engaged in your children's lives. Discuss their homework with them, attend their sporting events, participate in activities together, and talk to them about drugs. One of my pet peeves about our society today and many of the institutions that are helping to raise our children is that they don't make it easy for us to spend time with our own kids. For example, at the supposed "family YMCAs" near where we live, I've been very disappointed at how little of the facility, both in space and in available time, families can actually use. The YMCAs are frequently overrun by full-day "campers," left there by their parents, and kids enrolled in other drop-off programs.

6

THE SUPERSAVER:
HOARDING AND CHEATING

Anne Scheiber is the poster child for oversaving. Scheiber, despite earning modest wages during her working years as a government employee, passed away at the age of 101 with more than $20 million in assets. She did it through practicing the good financial habits of saving, starting at a young age, and investing in and holding on to a diversified portfolio of stocks.

Scheiber's story isn't uncommon in financial circles. In many ways, she epitomizes sound investing practices. However, what's especially notable about Scheiber's situation was that she chose to live in a cramped studio apartment and never lived off of her investments, not even their income. In retirement, she only used her small social security check and modest pension from her employer. Scheiber was extreme in her frugality and obsessed with her savings. "She had few friends. . . . [S]he was an unhappy person, totally consumed by her securities accounts and her money," reported an article about her in the *Washington Post*. Scheiber saved for the sake of saving without a goal or plan in mind and, frankly, without any benefit to herself.

Though somewhat extreme in her excessive saving, Scheiber is far from unique in my experience as a financial counselor. In fact, I've come across a surprising number of people who have a "problem" with saving too much and spending too little. That's why I say that we're not only a nation of overspenders; some of us are also oversavers. This chapter will discuss why "enough" isn't for some people, and not just exceptional cases like Scheiber. People who are good at saving money (or those who live with them and love them) will benefit from reading this chapter even if they are sure that they're not hoarders.

I touch on cheating in this chapter as well, which is a related, although different, behavior and has adverse long-term consequences in how we relate to money and others. Cheaters often feel a sense of entitlement to growing their nest eggs faster than what could be accomplished through simply being honest. Although cheaters are usually hoarders, they face the added challenge of changing their law-breaking behaviors and, in the worst cases, dealing with legal troubles. In concluding this chapter, I present specific strategies for coming to terms with hoarding behavior and reinforcing financial "honesty."

The Supersaver Personality

In my professional life, I've come across many cases of people who quite simply save too much and are overly concerned with forever amassing a bigger nest egg. I'll get to some case studies in a moment, but first I'd like to share my observations about common characteristics among money hoarders. These traits also apply to cheaters. (Please note my choice of the word *common* here; these are admittedly generalizations and don't always apply.)

Just as some people think that their financial problems will be solved if only they could earn a higher income, many oversavers believe that if they could reach a certain level of assets, they'd be more relaxed and do what they really want with their lives. The bar, however, continually gets raised, and the level of "enough" is rarely attained. For this reason, some of the best savers also have the most difficulty spending their money, even in retirement.

Supersavers and hoarders tend to have great insecurities relating to money. Specifically, they view amassing financial assets as providing them with safety and security that extend far beyond the financial realm. Although having more financial assets, in theory, provides greater financial peace of mind, these riches don't necessarily provide more of the other types of security for which hoarders are searching.

Plenty of money hoarders I've known over the years tend to be lonely, isolated people. They typically have few friends and passions. When money hoarders marry people with significantly different money personalities, fireworks ensue and divorce is often the result. Financial security doesn't translate into emotional security and contentment.

Achieving a certain level of affluence can provide for greater access to quality health care in the United States. However, once one reaches the point at which quality health care is the norm, the incessant pursuit of more money can have a negative impact on the individual's long-term health and quality of life. For example, supersavers often believe that they will be better protected as seniors and better able to enjoy their retirement years with hefty account balances. But the pursuit of more money, which typically entails longer work hours and greater stress, can lead to increased health problems in retirement years.

Interestingly, many supersavers (and overachieving workaholics, with whom supersavers share many traits) come from homes and families where they felt on the edge economically and emotionally. Although there are so many things that we can't control in the world, hoarders typically derive a tremendous sense of both economic and emotional security from saving a lot of money. And they love watching their money grow, although they have trouble with investing in volatile wealth-building investments like stocks because they generally abhor losing money even more.

Money hoarders have an amazing ability to selectively hear particular stories that reinforce rather than question their tendencies and beliefs. For example, stories periodically surface about how the legions of baby boomers retiring will bankrupt social security and cause a stock market collapse (more on this later in the chapter). Supersavers batten down the hatches, save more, and invest even more conservatively when such stories worry them. News stories about stock market declines, corporate layoffs, budget deficits, terrorism risks, rising oil prices, and conflicts in the Middle East and elsewhere cause supersavers to close their wallets, clutch their investments, and worry and save more. The lion's share of phone calls I fielded from my financial counseling clients came from worried supersavers who often found something on the evening news, in print, or online to worry about. And as any regular news junkie knows, there's plenty of negative, bad news available.

Too many financial advisers and planners have a tendency to heighten the anxieties of hoarders. One silly and inappropriate method I've seen some advisers use when creating a retirement plan is to tell their high-income clients that they need to save enough to replace, say, 90 percent of their current income throughout their retirement. A far lower percentage, which would necessitate saving a lot less money, may suit the client's long-term desires. Ultimately, the desired or needed percentage should be determined through retirement analysis of one's individual situation. I continue to be amazed at how often clients refuse to question the perceived wisdom that they should amass enough assets to replace such a large percentage of their income. Such advice can be self-serving for the adviser, as it creates even greater dependency on the part of the client for their continued counsel.

What follows are some case studies of typical supersavers I've worked with over the years. I've chosen these people because each one illustrates different issues, challenges, and solutions for money amassers (and cheaters). Later in the chapter, I'll also present additional advice for supersavers and those who love them—or have to deal with them!

Case Study: Dee

Dee got out of debt quickly after medical school. When she came to me for advice at the age of forty, she had only $16,000 remaining to be paid off on her home mortgage and had accumulated a hefty investment portfolio. She described herself as "frugal and prudent to the level of paranoia." After reading some of my books, she came to ask herself, and then me, an excellent question, "Am I saving too much?"

Dee came to this point of introspection about her life and work because she was considering taking an extended leave to perform volunteer medical work overseas. As she put it, "I don't want to die with $15 million in the bank and miss out on life-expanding opportunities." Financially speaking, what perplexed her was whether she could take a hiatus from saving money. She felt very uncomfortable doing so until she came across some of my writings. At the time, her financial assets totaled about $1 million.

You can find plenty of financial advisers, affluent people, as well as others who think $1 million isn't "enough" and not worth nearly what it used to be. However, $1 million in financial assets is a heck of a lot of money to have accumulated, especially by age forty and especially for someone like Dee who lived in the Midwest, an area of the country that offers a relatively moderate cost of living. I know plenty of retired folks who live quite happily with that amount of money or less.

Like many supersavers I've come to know, Dee didn't know how much new money she was actually saving annually. She was focused on her career and rarely set aside time to consider the bigger-picture financial issues. We were both surprised when she and I analyzed her finances to find that Dee was socking away 30 percent (about $90,000) of her yearly $200,000 salary. Given her relatively high tax bracket, Dee's savings rate is even more astounding. She actually was saving about two-thirds of her after-tax take-home pay—that's huge! (Dee's monthly mortgage payment was a mere $400, and her total expenditures came to less than $50,000 per year.)

Although she enjoys her chosen work as a physician, Dee was drained. She doesn't like her current boss, works twelve-hour days, and often works evenings and weekends at home. She estimates that she puts in seventy hours per week but is quick to point out that she gets a lot of joy from work, so she doesn't feel like a workaholic. (The fact that she gets a lot of joy from working so much doesn't prove she isn't a workaholic; in fact, she may have those tendencies, but that's a different topic dealt with in Chapter 3.)

She says that she would love to take a couple of years off but has been reluctant to do so, stating, "I've been a security-first person and want to have enough saved and be able to return to the same job, income, and ability to save more money." One of the reasons she continues to postpone her dream of doing overseas volunteer activities is that she'll likely never be guaranteed the same income and job upon her return. In speaking with her over time, however, she came to agree with me that she didn't know any unemployed physicians and that she wouldn't have much trouble replicating her current job, elements of which she didn't love anyway.

Dee's family background and upbringing are interesting and revealing. Her parents divorced when she was twelve years old. "My father had been a meticulous record keeper and financial manager. I needed to help my mom manage the household finances. I was doing the taxes for my mom at age fourteen. We balanced the checkbook together. Mom really needed my help. The thing that saved us was having a small mortgage—$108 per month," says Dee. Reflecting upon her childhood, she feels that these early years imparted a sense of insecurity and lack of control that she still wrestles with in adulthood, "not because we got creditor calls or because I was deprived. We had no buffer for disasters or security." Dee was emotionally as well as financially deprived, and she missed out on a lot of childhood happiness. Now, as an adult, she seeks to exert control over her life through amassing a large nest egg, which can't provide emotional happiness and security.

My advice to Dee was that she shouldn't postpone what she really wanted to do. She was saving a lot and had very low expenditures in relation to her income. She worked in a high demand, secure profession and would surely find comparable work upon her return from overseas. I also helped Dee do some basic retirement analysis that enabled her to see how well off she was simply on the basis of what she'd saved already at the tender age of forty. When I last spoke with her, she commented,

"I need to loosen up and see the world and enjoy myself and the planet. Thou shalt travel!"

Case Study: James

When I first met James, he was a highly successful executive in his late thirties. He was pulling down about $1 million annually and had already piled up a multimillion-dollar net worth. James worked very long hours and, as a result, was developing some related health problems. When we began discussing his situation, he reported that he had never made a financial decision that he was pleased with. He rarely dated and, by his own admission, had few friends.

When we discussed his short-term and long-term financial and personal goals, James stated that he wanted to maximize the potential return of his portfolio without losing money. It wasn't obvious to James that these two conflicting objectives weren't really possible to achieve. James's feelings on this issue highlight a common problem that supersavers have with investing. Many of them have great difficulty placing even modest portions of their money into the more conservative of vehicles that offer growth potential, such as stock mutual funds. If they do take the plunge into slightly volatile waters, they quickly bail when prices go down.

After working with James for a period of time, I came to learn that he had more than $1 million dollars in one bank account! In addition to the low returns this account provided, he hadn't realized the risk to which he was exposed. The FDIC insurance on one bank account is just $100,000. Thus, if his bank happened to fail (and banks do fail), he was at risk of losing all the money in the account in excess of $100,000.

One of James's longer-term goals was to achieve "financial freedom" by the age of fifty by accumulating about $10 million. He did indeed accomplish this goal, and, no surprise to me, it wasn't enough to satiate his desire to work and accumulate greater savings. He then turned to new worries after reaching the $10 million mark. He's now concerned about news reports of higher than expected oil prices and outliving his money. The bar keeps getting set higher and higher. So James continues to work hard, save a lot, and not spend.

In my initial years working with James, I wasn't really able to help him with his problem of oversaving, and the reasons behind that fact are interesting and thought provoking. I had very limited interactions with him during this period. When he first consulted with me, I was frankly unaware of this problem that he had. In retrospect, I can see that part of the issue was that he did a masterful job of concealing some of his savings! He originally engaged my services simply to provide some investment advice on a retirement account. He wanted to invest the money in better-returning vehicles than a bank account, but he was fearful of moving out of the bank account.

James really needed the kind of professional counseling assistance that a sharp psychologist could provide. In his late forties, his lifelong financial habits were quite ingrained. I took the risk in suggesting to James that he work with a psychologist after he provided me an opening one day when he lamented his lack of a romantic relationship and the historic problems that he had with women. After working with a counselor for about a year, James arrived back on my doorstep, and we finally began to make some headway with his saving addiction and resistance to investing less conservatively. The biggest contribution from his counseling was that it enabled him to "see" how his long work hours and unrelenting focus on amassing money were causing him to be unhappy and fail at interpersonal relationships.

After I was finally able to get him to sit down with an open mind to work with me in reviewing the current state of his retirement planning, James became far more comfortable that he had already accumulated a lot of money to provide a nice standard of living down the road. Paying off his home mortgage, which was easy for him to do, also made him feel at greater ease with his financial situation. As he learned about different investments and the risks (including exposure to inflation and taxes) that he was incurring by keeping so much of his cash in bank accounts, he was far more receptive to diversify with some growth investments like stock and real estate.

Case Study: Michelle

I was initially struck by Michelle's assertive, take-no-prisoners manner (her personality reminded me somewhat of Martha Stewart). Michelle was doing very well in her career and was saving a lot of money. She was quite proud of her burgeoning investment balances, and she wanted a lot more future growth. She hinted that she was "aggressive" in preparing her personal income tax returns. Over the years, I began to learn what Michelle meant by that phrase: she inflated her deductions and didn't report all of her self-employment income. In other words, she was cheating. Ultimately, she landed in trouble with the IRS, was audited, incurred some stiff penalties, and was lucky not to do jail time given the amount of cheating she had done.

Michelle was well educated and accomplished in her profession. She earned more than $100,000 annually and didn't "need" to cheat to make ends meet. Michelle cheated, it seemed, mostly from insecurities about her future. She worried that she may not be as employable or that her income would drop substantially in the future. She resented how much she had to pay in taxes and didn't want to have to work longer hours to make and save more money.

Her desires to amass more money also led her to bend the truth about other aspects in her life that had a financial component, such as product returns and orders that she made. She admitted to me on several occasions to returning products outside of their warranty periods and lying about when she bought them. I also found in my interactions with her that she often angled to get something for nothing and not pay for all of the services rendered. As I was forced to do on rare occasion, I quietly made myself unavailable for future consultations with her to keep from being taken advantage of.

Michelle was a sad and empty person who didn't connect with people. She was devoted to her career and accumulating money and not much else. She never raised topics that would've naturally led me into a discussion with her about recognizing and dealing with her problems. I'm no psychologist, but it was pretty obvious to me that Michelle needed some enjoyable activities outside of her work that would enable her to meet and connect with others.

Case Study: Rick and Debby

Rick and Debby were in an adult education class that I used to teach. They were an energetic and attentive couple. When I told the class that, as a matter of policy, I did not want to have students calling me at the end of the course to engage my services as a financial counselor, Rick and Debby promptly dropped out of the class and called my office. (I feel that it is an enormous conflict of interest when "teachers" teach for the purpose of cultivating financial-advisory clients.) Despite my best efforts to convince them to stay in the class and learn how to better manage their money through completing the course, they became clients instead.

Rick and Debby both worked as full-time professionals in their chosen fields and were high-income earners. Now in their late forties, they had foregone the opportunity to have children partly because of their devotion to their careers. They were able to save large portions of their annual combined incomes—on the order of 35 percent and more. Although they were leery of the stock market, Rick and Debby owned a number of real-estate investment properties. Despite owning a half-dozen well-located and modest-size single-family homes to accompany their near million dollars in other financial assets, Rick and Debby felt far from financially secure.

This couple had an amazing ability to see the glass as half empty rather than half full. Despite the hundreds of thousands of dollars in equity in all of the properties they owned, they dwelled on their feelings that they had bought several of them "near the top of the market." And despite their blue-chip educational credentials and successful careers, they worried incessantly about being laid off and never being rehired. The better I got to know Rick and Debby, the more disturbed I became that, like Michelle, they cheated on their taxes. They seemed somewhat embarrassed to admit this but were comfortable enough with this behavior (and me) to discuss the situation.

Over time, I was able to show Ricky and Debby how well off they were with their investments. As the years passed, I kept reminding them how well their investments were appreciating and that the mortgages on their rental properties were being paid down while the homes were gaining in value. Performing a thorough retirement analysis and periodically updating the information helped them feel much better about the standard of living that their assets would provide. Debby scaled back her work responsibilities, and they eventually ended up adopting two children. They found that they loved being parents and working less.

Overcoming Oversaving

I'm not going to claim that changing ingrained habits associated with hoarding money and cheating comes easily. However, I have had the opportunity and enjoyment of helping numerous money amassers overcome their excessive ways. Conquering oversaving and an obsession with money typically requires a mix of education and specific incremental behavioral changes. Substantive change typically comes over months and years, not days and weeks.

Understand the Link between Money and Happiness

Quite a lot of research has been conducted not only in the United States but also worldwide examining the link, or lack thereof, between affluence and happiness. In a study conducted by psychology professors Richard Ryan and Timothy Kasser, more than 1,000 people were interviewed in thirteen countries. Through questionnaires, researchers were able to measure how important (extrinsic) materialistic values such as image, status, and financial success were to various people and then measure these folks' psychological happiness. Ryan and Kasser found that having more money, in and of itself, did not increase people's happiness or cause problems.

The obsessive pursuit of wealth and adoption of money as one's primary motivator, however, led to psychological unhappiness, severe depression, anxiety, and other problems, including a far higher incidence of alcohol, drug, and tobacco abuse. Kasser, the author of *The High Price of Materialism* (MIT Press), has himself conducted extensive research into this topic and compiled many studies. In reference to others' studies, Kasser states, "The results consistently pointed towards the conclusion that materialistic people were less happy and satisfied with life, and that they also reported more distress. Thus, the more people buy into the messages of consumer society, the lower their levels of personal well-being and the higher their levels of distress."

Robert Lane, author of *The Loss of Happiness in Market Democracies* (Yale University Press), has conducted extensive research in the field of money and life satisfaction and has found that the primary sources of long-term happiness are friends and family. "Amidst the satisfaction people feel with material progress, there is a spirit of unhappiness and depression haunting advanced market democracies throughout the world. . . . Once you get past the poverty level, there's no correlation between increased wealth and greater happiness. If anything, it's quite the reverse."

Studies of twins, which often provide valuable insights, concur with Lane's conclusions. Drs. David Likken and Auke Tellegen found in their research in a University of Minnesota twins' project that a mere 2 percent of the differences in happiness among people can be attributed to differences in income.

Psychology professor Dr. David Myers has studied happiness for decades. He has found that wealth, gender, age, education, and occupation do not determine happiness. What he has found leads people to be happy are optimism, self-esteem, a sense of personal control, and extroversion. People also derive happiness from investing in friendships and family ties, being with people with whom they can openly share and talk about themselves. "Having food, shelter and safety is basic to our well being. But once able to afford life's necessities, increasing levels of affluence matter surprisingly little. Wealth is like health: Although its absence can breed misery, having it is no guarantee of happiness," writes Myers. Note Myers's choice of the word *necessities.* In my experience working with and observing people, it's clear to me that many Americans have lost sight of the differences between necessities and luxuries, especially in affluent and upper-middle-class communities. We can always find people with bigger homes and more expensive cars and who have taken more exotic vacations. The bar is continually set higher and higher in terms of how much money we "need."

A business acquaintance of mine, whom I'll refer to as Mark, presents what I think is an absurd extreme in this regard. He works in the investment field, puts in horrendous hours, and is a multimillionaire. Based on conversations that I've had with him, his net worth is at least $5 million and probably as much as $10 million. Mark grew up in a middle-class family that often struggled to make ends meet. In his forties, he has a family but sees very little of them. Mark is an extremely competent businessman but a workaholic who doesn't feel the least bit financially secure. For years, he even balked at buying a modest home, which his wife really wanted to do so the family could settle down with the kids and not be subject to the whims of a landlord. If he wanted to, he could retire and shift careers to spend more time with his wife and kids and on his hobbies. But he

LETTING GO OF
BABY-BOOMER FEARS

One justification that supersavers use for their actions is the litany of fears surrounding the tens of millions of baby boomers hitting retirement age around the same time. The story goes that retiring boomers will cause a mammoth collapse of the stock market as they sell out to finance their golden years. Real estate prices are supposed to plummet as well, as everyone sells their larger homes and retires to small condominiums in the Sun Belt.

Such doomsaying about the future of financial and real estate markets is unfounded. The fear that boomers will suddenly sell everything when they hit retirement is bogus. Nobody sells off his entire nest egg the day after he stops working; retirement can last up to thirty years, and assets are depleted quite gradually. On top of that, boomers vary in age by up to sixteen years and, thus, will be retiring at different times. The wealthiest (who hold the bulk of real estate and stocks) won't even sell most of their holdings but will, like the wealthy of previous generations, pass on many of their assets.

doesn't. Mark doesn't feel the least bit financially secure. He truly believes that he needs $20 million to be financially comfortable. $20 million!

Which bring me back to my favorite quote from Dr. David Myers, which is apropos to Mark: "Satisfaction isn't so much getting what you want but wanting what you have. There are two ways to be rich: one is to have great wealth, the other is to have few wants." Supersavers, like Mark and others discussed in this chapter, to their detriment latch on to the former definition. The next section covers how hoarders can make the transition to have fewer wants (and worries).

Learn to Work Less, Save Less, and Spend More

The vast majority of supersavers whom I've worked with and observed work too many hours and neglect their loved ones and themselves. In short, most of them are also workaholics. They should strive to work less and lead more balanced lives. Because that's the subject of Chapter 3, I'm not going to cover the same ground here, but please closely review that material, especially the recommendation section. Instead, I want to help you loosen those purse strings. Learning to spend more and save less is a problem more Americans wish they had, so consider yourself lucky in that regard. Try the following strategies to enable you to give yourself permission to spend more:

Review some realistic projections of what standard of living can be provided by the assets you've already accumulated. This is one of my favorite exercises to use with supersavers. Many people whom I've worked with have been pleasantly surprised by this analysis. There are numerous useful retirement-planning worksheets and analytic tools you can use to assess where you currently stand in terms of saving for retirement. My favorites are the printed work booklets offered by T. Rowe Price (1-800-638-5660) and their online tools (http://www.troweprice.com), along with the Web tools available at http://www.vanguard.com.

Go on a news diet. Minimize and even avoid news programs that dwell on the negative, which will only reinforce your fears about never having enough money.

Regularly (as in once a week or once a month) buy something that you historically have viewed as frivolous but you can truly afford. Treat yourself! By all means, spend the money on something that brings you the most joy, whether it's eating out occasionally at a pricey restaurant or taking an extra vacation during the year.

Buy more gifts for the people you love. Money hoarders actually tend to be more generous with loved ones than they are with themselves. However, oversavers still tend to squelch their desires to buy gifts or help out those they care about. Likewise, loosening the purse strings on family members is an important step. How would you like it if a family member or close friend followed you around all day and totaled up the number of calories that you consumed? Well, then, why would you expect your family to happily accept your daily, weekly, and monthly tracking of their expenditures?

For people having difficulty saving enough toward their financial goals, a spending inventory can yield tremendous benefits. However, that doesn't mean that continually tracking expenses is the best approach to managing household finances for everyone, especially for folks with a propensity to save a lot. People who most benefit from assessing where their money goes each month are those who spend more than they earn or who save too little. What's too little? To be able to accomplish common financial goals, such as retiring in your sixties, most people should save at least 5 to 10 percent of their pretax income.

You may not know how much of your income you should be saving to accomplish your goals. Perhaps you haven't established clear goals or you haven't calculated how much you truly need to save to achieve them. After you determine the portion of your income that you should be saving and you're able to save at least that much, you don't have to regularly track your spending—or your family members'. (Just be sure that you're not masking overspending through the accumulation of consumer debt.)

In some families, supersavers who habitually track their spending drive everyone else crazy with their money monitoring. Personal finances become a constant source of unnecessary stress and anxiety. Especially if you're automatically saving money from each paycheck or saving on a monthly basis, does it really matter where the rest of it goes? (Of course, none of us want family members to engage in illegal or harmful behaviors. But other than that, enjoy life.)

Work at establishing guidelines and a culture of spending money that everyone can agree and live with. For example, some couples I know discuss only larger purchases, which are defined as exceeding a certain dollar limit such as one hundred or two hundred dollars. Parents who teach their children about spending wisely pass along far more valuable financial lessons than do elders who nag and complain about specific purchases. (Chapter 8 covers the often prickly topic of money and relationships, and Chapter 9 provides tips on raising money-wise children.)

Remember: If you're accomplishing your savings goals, go easier on yourself and family when it comes to everyday expenses. You'll all be happier for it.

DEALING WITH SUDDEN WEALTH— WINDFALLS AND INHERITANCES

The biggest irony in regard to people pursuing large sums of money is that, more often than not, those who come into substantial money discover that life isn't "better" for them. Folks who come by their wealth suddenly, such as through an inheritance or winning the lottery, are often surprised at the stress and problems that accompany their newfound riches. Sudden wealth doesn't make one's days blissful and free of worry—quite the opposite in many cases.

For starters, people who've fretted about money and believed that having more money would make their lives so much better typically find that their lives don't magically improve when they have greater financial assets. Interestingly, people who experience windfalls find dissatisfaction with the rest of their lives.

If you have great wealth, you must be especially careful about passing on too much to your children. Excessive assets can lead your kids to be lazy, lack purpose, and do nothing with their lives.

The key to making the most of your wealth is to keep in mind what money can buy—choices, freedom, and options but only if you recognize that and take advantage of it. For example, most parents wish they had more time for their kids and themselves. If you have come into a financial windfall, you can work less and have more time, yet few people take advantage of this opportunity.

Invest Intelligently

As discussed earlier, supersavers often have trouble moving into growth-oriented investments and sticking with them because they abhor losing money. Please be sure to read the section "Conquering Your Stock-Investing Fears" in Chapter 4.

THE AVOIDER: MONEY AVOIDANCE AND DISORGANIZATION

"I didn't open an investment statement for nearly two years. In the past when I reviewed my investments, my stomach got in knots and I felt tremendous anxiety and tension," Susan told me as we reviewed her investment portfolio. Much of Susan's money was sitting in a money market fund, and the remainder was in GNMA (mortgage-backed) bonds that she didn't understand and felt intimated about. "My broker, who I inherited through a relative, rarely called . . . probably because he knew better! I never made decisions and was plagued by discomfort with just about any investment. I'm ashamed to say that I couldn't even tell you how much I have invested just now or where it all is," she sheepishly told me.

Almost all of us avoid dealing with some aspect of money. For some, it's as simple as avoiding balancing a checkbook or making decisions about where to invest saved money. Others neglect needed insurance coverage, perhaps out of fear of confronting their own mortality and vulnerabilities. Some people are plagued by broader problems such as feelings of guilt and shame about money or feeling that money seems dirty and evil.

This chapter discusses the roots of avoidance issues and how to overcome procrastination. Along the way, I present sure steps to getting organized.

Signs and Symptoms

I will confess to avoiding some aspects of dealing with money. Over the years, I've found it kind of humorous, actually, that many people assume that because I write financial-advice books and columns and have worked as a financial counselor, I must maintain meticulous financial records, including regularly balancing my checkbook. The reality is that I abhor and despise the minutiae of balancing checkbooks and tracking other little, picky details. My feelings on this matter are likely the result of growing up with a father who was a mechanical engineer. He loved and even wallowed in details and minutiae. His teaching methods often drove me crazy because he was such a micromanager.

I got a lot of mail from readers the first time I admitted to not balancing my checkbook. Such a confession didn't fit well with the image that many people wanted to have of me as this all-knowing, all-in-control, detail-oriented, financial-loving sort of guy. The fact is that I do enjoy numbers and analysis and thinking about financial strategy. But I detest spending hours of my time on the tedium of making all the dollars and pennies balance precisely in my checking account register. I'm satisfied with the portion of income that I save each month and have low-cost overdraft protection on the checking account in the unlikely event the account runs dry. That's more than good enough for me. But this approach isn't for everyone. Some people face high fees if they bounce a check from overdrawing

WHY SOME PEOPLE DON'T NEED TO BALANCE THEIR CHECKBOOKS

When I've explained to people why I don't balance my checkbook and the fact that I don't incur large bounced check fees, I still get those who say that I should be balancing my checkbook to catch bank errors. Banks, of course, aren't perfect. However, in all my years in the financial business, I've *never* met or heard of anyone who regularly finds large errors in their checking account balance. But suppose that by virtue of balancing your checkbook regularly, you find a $100 error once a year. Here's how much you're making per hour for your balancing efforts: Logging all of the transactions and balancing your account takes at least a couple of hours per month. So if you were to find a $100 error once a year, your effective hourly compensation would be about $4.17, which is less than minimum-wage jobs at fast food joints.

Now bouncing checks costs some people hundreds of dollars annually, if they bounce checks a few times per year. So if you're in that camp, you should be balancing your checkbook. You might also look into overdraft protection that could greatly reduce the costs of such episodes. (Some discount brokerage accounts offering unlimited check writing provide low-cost margin loans as overdraft protection.) If you live on a tight budget, keep low account balances, and can't afford the cost of overdraft protection, by all means regularly balance your checkbook register and keep a running total of your account balance.

their account, or they're unable to keep a sufficient cushion in their account to ensure that they rarely face a situation in which overdrafts occur. I'm not recommending my approach across the board; I'm simply demonstrating the fact that most of us avoid some aspect of dealing with our finances.

In my work as a financial counselor, I saw plenty of money avoiders. Some of these people hired me in the hopes of helping them get a grip on their financial situation. More often than not, avoiders didn't recognize their underlying problems but instead contacted me because of a current quandary—such as wanting to buy a home and not feeling comfortable with how much to spend. My challenge was to gently get folks to realize the larger issues and little details that were being ignored.

Here are a few of the more concrete physical signs and symptoms I often saw that indicated I was dealing with someone who was a money avoider:

Disorganization and clutter.   Because avoiders dislike dealing with money and related issues, they certainly don't spend their free time keeping documents organized and easy to find.

Late bills and tax payments.   Money avoiders often incur late fees and interest charges on various household bills. Those who are self-employed and responsible for quarterly income tax filings are at additional risk for falling behind with tax payments, the negative financial consequences of which can be huge.

Unopened account statements.   We all get busy with life, but I was amazed at how many money avoiders I worked with who had piles of unopened account statements, even during periods when their types of investments were doing fine, thus eliminating any reason for avoiding opening potentially bad news.

As for the fiscal and mental symptoms, the following are common in my experience:

A sense of unease, and even shame and embarrassment, with having cash sitting around in low-interest accounts. Money avoiders who are able to save money may have a tendency to allow it to accumulate, for example, in bank accounts that pay little if any interest. Although they may know that they could and should do better with investing the money, they can't overcome the inertia.

Feelings of enormous stress and anxiety over money issues and decisions. One of the main reasons that avoiders relate to money in the way that they do is because for whatever historic reason(s), making financial decisions makes them feel very uncomfortable and stressed. (In some cases, for example, growing up in a home where money was an ongoing source of unhappiness, conflicts, and problems can lead to avoidance behavior as an adult.) Other people believe that they lack the skills and knowledge necessary to take control of their finances. Finally, some folks believe, rightly or wrongly, that their current financial picture isn't so bright, so they simply decide to avoid the bad news, even though ignoring the situation will make things only worse in the end.

Low level of interest over money issues and decisions. Whereas some avoiders shun financial decisions and responsibilities due to anxiety, others are imitating behavior learned from their parents or are rebelling against a parent who was financially or emotionally overbearing.

An absence of long-term planning and thinking. Many of the money avoiders I dealt with clearly hadn't thought much of what their personal and financial goals were for the years and decades ahead.

Marriage problems.   Money avoiders typically have conflicts over money with their spouses, and their avoidance may stem from or be exacerbated by that issue.

When a new potential client contacted me, in addition to explaining my services and fees, I would ask some general background questions about the person's financial situation. Prior to the first in-person meeting with new clients, I'd mail a detailed questionnaire for them to complete. Occasionally, I'd meet with a client who hadn't filled out any of the form (or just a small portion of it) and who had to continuously get up and go searching through the house for missing documents and unopened envelopes. These folks were clearly avoiders. Even in the face of having to pay for more of my time, they couldn't bring themselves to deal with the questionnaire and paperwork collection and organization.

Why Avoiders Avoid

I'm not going to spend a lot of time on the topic of why avoiders avoid because it can quickly delve into complicated emotional and psychological topics. That said, understanding some of the common feelings and issues surrounding money-avoidance behavior can help in coming to acknowledge and productively change the habits. The typical reasons that some people are chronic money avoiders include:

Feelings of incompetence.   Some people have negative associations from prior attempts, with parents or spouses, at dealing with money and making financial decisions. Many money avoiders have similar feelings of incompetence with math and mathematical analysis, which are certainly key abilities to possess for effective personal financial management. Lack of experience in making financial decisions certainly plays into avoiders' feelings of incompetence as well.

Disorganization. Money avoiders have a tendency to be generally disorganized people who avoid dealing with other facets of their lives as well. With only so many hours in the day, people who are poorly organized struggle just to deal with work and family responsibilities. Making financial decisions, especially those dealing with longer-term issues (for example, retirement planning or insurance), is easily postponed or never considered.

Marital friction. As I will discuss in the next chapter, money is among the leading causes of marital discord. Some spouses cope by avoiding the topic altogether in the hopes of keeping more harmony in their marriages. In the short term, this avoidance strategy may reduce some stress and arguments. In the long term, however, it doesn't work, as dissatisfaction gone underground doesn't go away (or get better).

Afraid of bad things happening. People who were abused growing up or lived with a loved one who was a substance abuser often worry about bad things occurring. Ditto for folks suffering from depression or with generalized anxiety disorders. Money troubles are often intertwined with abuse issues in homes and lead to plenty of negative associations with money and simply not wanting to deal with the topic.

Perfectionism. Although this is a less common reason for people shunning money matters, some perfectionists continue putting off making decisions and taking action because they can always find flaws in or obstacles to their intended course of action, or they may feel that they might make a better decision with just a little more thinking and analysis.

Can get away with it. Some people simply don't want to deal with money issues and decisions and are able to get along sufficiently well enough through good fortune and being surrounded by those who enable the avoiding behavior (perhaps through caregiving and taking responsibility). Unfortunately, life changes and unforeseen problems can expose gaps in poor financial management, which is the topic of the next section.

Consequences of Avoiding

Some money avoiders can "get away" with their procrastinating ways for a number of years. However, whether it's in the short term or the long term, problems do eventually occur from avoiding dealing with money and related decisions, and sometimes the damage can be catastrophic.

A Reduced Standard of Living and Dislocations from Insurance Gaps

Insurance is an admittedly dreadful topic for most people (my apologies if you're in that line of business and you love it!). As a result, avoiding insurance-related issues ranks high among chronic money procrastinators. And even though well-intentioned and commission-hungry insurance agents get some people to plug most of their insurance gaps, these salespeople may not direct you to the policy best suited to your needs. In fact, brokers might sell you costly insurance (for instance, cash-value life insurance) that provides them with a higher take and you with less insurance than you might really need.

George, in his midforties, was his family's provider. He had four children, and his wife didn't work outside the home. Although he was a good wage earner, he and his wife were hopelessly disorganized when it came to managing their money, and they consistently avoided financial decisions and planning. They didn't save for retirement, they didn't have proper life and disability insurance, and they even lacked an adequate emergency cash buffer. One spring morning, George collapsed in his office and was rushed to a nearby hospital where he found out that he'd suffered a major heart attack. Six months later, he had another heart attack that, sadly, took his life and left his wife and children with a small life insurance policy that his employer provided as a basic benefit. The family was in financial and emotional turmoil from George's death and the resulting chaos caused by a lack of financial planning and his money avoidance. His widow lost their home in the next year. Due to cost considerations, the family was forced to move to another town; the kids then had to go through the difficult process of forging new friendships in a new school district on top of all the other emotional hardship that they were suffering.

Insurance gaps also come to light when a disability or a protracted illness occurs. Too often, we believe that these problems happen only to elderly people, but they don't. In fact, statistically, you are far more likely to miss work for an extended period of time due to a disability or lengthy illness than you are to pass away prematurely.

Working Later in Life Because of Insufficient Retirement Savings

Some money avoiders don't plan ahead and save toward future goals. Sadly, I've met with people in their forties and fifties who are just beginning to comprehend the consequences of such behavior. Often, the reality hits home when they contact the Social Security Administration (SSA) or get a mailing from the SSA and learn what size benefit check they'll get at full retirement age (which is around age sixty-six for most people). By *reality*, I mean the realization that they'll have to continue working into their seventies in order to maintain the modest standard of living to which they've become accustomed.

Several issues typically cause a lack of retirement funds:

Not saving enough. Many money avoiders could save more money, but they typically aren't motivated and organized enough to do so. Generally, they haven't bothered to conduct even basic retirement analysis to understand how much they should be saving to reach their retirement goal (or even think about when and if they wish to retire).

Low return on investment. Because money avoiders dislike dealing with money, what they're able to save often gets "ignored" and languishes in low- or no-interest bank accounts. Avoiders also tend to fall prey to the worst salespeople who push them into mediocre or poor investments with high fees.

Losing money due to poor investment selection and trading. This problem is often the result of falling into the clutches of the most unscrupulous salespeople who are more interested in making money for themselves than for you with your money. When avoiders choose their own investments, it's often done based on superficial research and analysis. Discomfort causes avoiders to bail out when things look bleak or to pile into frothy investments when they're very popular or both.

Family Chaos and Fighting Precipitated by Lack of Wills and Trusts

As we age, the percentage of people passing away gradually increases. The following table shows the mortality rate for various age ranges. You can see that whereas just 1 percent of those folks between the ages of twenty-five and thirty-four passes away each decade, the portion approximately doubles with each passing decade. Though one in one hundred is a relatively small probability, it's a much greater probability than winning your local megamillions jackpot. Between the ages of forty-five and fifty-four, nearly one in every twenty-five people passes away during a decade.

Age Range	Percentage of People Dying Each Decade
25–34	1.0
35–44	2.0
45–54	4.3
55–64	9.6
65–74	23.5
75–84	55.8

Money avoiders, more often than not, lack wills and other legal documents that should specify to whom various assets shall pass and who is responsible for what (for example, administrating the estate and raising minor children) in the event of their untimely demise. When money is to pass to heirs through an estate, the absence of documents can lead to major legal and family battles.

Advice for Conquering Money Avoidance and Disorganization

If you or someone you love is a money avoider, my goal isn't to turn you or them into someone who loves dealing with money. That's not going to happen. However, we can work together to ensure that you can accomplish common financial goals and won't suffer the ill effects that money avoiders so often do in their neglect of their finances.

Making Changes—Gradually and Steadily

Coming to terms with money avoidance takes time—often a lot of time and patience. That statement isn't meant to provide you with a reason to continue to forgo making changes in your financial life. Instead, I'm relaying a fact and reminding you that change takes time and some steps forward interrupted by steps back.

The first and most important part in the process is to recognize the tendency and some of the biggest causes. Many people find it helpful and insightful to speak with someone who is an empathic listener about their feelings and history with money or to write down their feelings relating to money avoidance. "I always felt stupid about math and wholly inadequate. I can't even bring myself to use a calculator out of fear I won't even know how to use that properly," says Heidi, a forty-something-year-old woman. It took Heidi about two years to make some major changes in how she handled her personal finances. She began to make progress when I was able to persuade her that she didn't have to be a math whiz to make positive financial changes. Heidi didn't have major spending problems, but she was sloppy and lazy about saving money and investing it well.

I had her sign up for her employer's retirement savings plan so that she could begin to save about 8 percent of her salary. We had the money withdrawn from her salary and directed into a handful of well-diversified mutual funds. "I can't believe how painless it is to do this, and there was virtually no math involved. All I had to do was complete a one-page enrollment form, which required me to say what funds and what percentage of my contribution went into each fund that I selected," said Heidi. With the meager amounts she had been saving that were languishing in a low-interest bank account, Heidi would've needed to work until her midseventies to achieve the standard of living in retirement that she desired. Now, she's on track to be able to stop working by her late fifties. Seeing these quantifiable changes in her retirement age and gaining a basic understanding of the steps she needs to take to reach her goals has been a great motivating source to Heidi and has given her savings a purpose. Equally if not more important, she feels in control of her life, financially, and rid herself of that ever-constant underlying anxiety about not being on top of things.

I found that many avoiders typically felt greatly overwhelmed with a laundry list of financial to-dos. That's why you should prioritize and work on only the top one or two items at a time. I'd tell clients that even though they might have a total of eight or ten things on their longer task lists, they shouldn't expect to complete those next week or even next month. It might take them six months to a year to work through the longer list.

Dealing with Bills and Debts

People who are financially disorganized and avoid dealing with money often are late paying bills. Late payments, particularly when it comes to paying taxes, are a problem that can lead to substantial late fees, interest, and penalties. Even if the fees and additional interest from individual late payments—five dollars here and thirty dollars there—don't seem all that significant on their own, they can add up to a significant total if you make paying bills late a habit.

One of the best things that a money avoider can do with their bills is to set each of them up for automatic payment. Whether it's your phone, utility, or monthly mortgage bill, you should be able to establish an automatic payment plan that doesn't require you to initiate payment. With just a little up-front work with each creditor or billing company—often not much more effort than paying a monthly bill—you can rid yourself of unnecessary fees and interest and save a little time each month. Many companies accept (and actually prefer) payment through an electronic transfer from your bank account. Some loan holders (such as the U.S. Department of Education) may even lessen your interest rate slightly in return for what amounts to a guarantee of an on-time payment every month. If not, you may be able to have the payment charged to your credit card, but be careful with this route if you sometimes don't pay that bill in full and on time!

If, for whatever reason, you're unable or unwilling to put your bills on an automatic payment system, you can put together an accordion-style folder and organize your bills based on when during the month they need to be paid. Please understand that I think this system is second-rate (in terms of efficiency and likelihood for success) compared with an automatic payment system.

Developing a Regular Investment Program

Just as Heidi did, all money avoiders should make their investing automatic. If you work for an employer, doing so is usually pretty easy. Often, the most daunting part of the process is wading through the wad of retirement plan and investment information and brochures your benefits department may dump on you when you tell them that you want to sign up for their payroll-deduction savings program. Not only will your money grow faster inside a tax-deferred account, but your employer may also be offering you free matching money.

The simplest way to navigate through the morass of paperwork is to look first for the specific form you must complete to sign up for the payroll investment program. Thoroughly read that form first so that you know what you need to focus on and get smarter about as you pore over all of the other materials.

If your earnings come from self-employment income, you'll need to establish your own retirement account. Learn about the different retirement-account options and choose the one that best meets your needs. The two self-employed retirement-account options that enable you to sock away the greatest amounts are SEP-IRAs and Keoghs. With each of these plans, a self-employed person may contribute up to 20 percent of his or business's net income up to a maximum of more than $40,000 (contact an investment firm or tax adviser for the current dollar limit). These plans may be established through the major mutual fund companies that I like such as Vanguard, Fidelity, and T. Rowe Price. And you can generally set up these accounts so that a regular monthly amount is zapped electron-ically from your local bank account into your mutual-fund in-vestment account.

Closing Insurance Gaps

Nearly every money avoider I've met over the years has prob-lematic gaps in their insurance coverage. Solving this problem presents some challenges because understanding various poli-cies and coverages is complicated enough; then, add on top of that the unfortunate fact that to buy most insurance policies, you must deal with a commission-based insurance agent. Talk about a recipe for headaches and conflicts of interest! But these are not acceptable excuses for avoiding this issue because so much is at stake. So, for each of the following types of policies, I explain who needs it and how to get the coverage you need at a competitive price:

Health insurance.   Everyone needs a comprehensive so-called major medical policy. Money avoiders, especially those who are young, may think that they don't need health insurance as long as they're healthy. Problem is, none of us knows when life will throw us a medical curveball. To keep the cost to a more reason-able (less ridiculous) level, buy a health insurance policy with high deductibles (the initial expenses you are required to pay out of your own pocket). As you shop among health insurance plans, give preference to those offered by the biggest and longest-standing insurers in the health insurance arena such as Aetna, Anthem, Assurant, Blue Cross, Blue Shield, Kaiser, and UnitedHealthcare. An insurance agent who specializes in health insurance may be of assistance to you, but be aware that agents derive a commission based on the amount of your premiums, so this presents agents with a conflict of interest not to advocate lower-cost plans and plan options.

Long-term disability insurance. Most people's greatest financial "asset" is their ability to earn future employment income. However, outside of people working for larger employers with comprehensive benefit plans, many lack long-term disability insurance. Good places to start searching for such coverage are professional associations that you currently belong to or could join based on your occupation or training. USAA Life (1-800-531-8000) offers competitive disability plans from other carriers (and thus acts as a broker).

Term life insurance. When others are dependent on your employment income, you should carry life insurance coverage. The amount of the term life insurance you buy should be determined based on how many years' worth of your income you seek to replace. For example, if you have young children and desire to replace your income over the next twenty years, you would multiply your after-tax annual income by fifteen. So if you're after-tax income is $40,000 yearly, you should buy a $600,000 term life policy. For competitive term life insurance quotes, contact TD Waterhouse Insurance Services at 1-800-622-3699 and USAA Life at 1-800-531-8000.

Being Especially Careful Hiring Financial Help

Money avoiders are clearly a group of people who could benefit from hiring a financial adviser. However, they're also among the people most likely to make a poor choice when hiring. It's difficult to evaluate or care enough to evaluate the financial expertise (and potential conflicts of interest) of a financial adviser if you're uninterested in (or suffer anxiety about) and actively avoid money issues.

Your first step, if you're inclined to hire help, is to clearly define what it is that you desire assistance with. Do you need assistance with analyzing your budget and developing a plan to pay down consumer debt? If so, most financial advisers aren't really trained for or interested in helping you with that (there's far more money to be made selling investment and insurance products to the affluent). If you're looking to wipe out debt and analyze your household budget, please see my suggestions in Chapter 2. Advisers are best suited for folks who want to quantify how much they should be saving for specific goals and determining where to invest it.

However, there's no getting around it: you do have to do a lot of digging to find a competent and ethical adviser who has reasonable fees. With that information in hand, you can confidently and strategically evaluate potential service providers who can help you overcome your inertia and get you on track to managing your money.

CONFLICT, NEGOTIATION, AND COMPROMISE: RELATIONSHIPS AND MONEY

In the earlier chapters in this book, I've focused on a variety of problems that people have with their own money habits. Although overspending, overworking, addictions, and poor investing habits clearly affect other family members and relatives on many levels, I've not yet explicitly dealt with how we relate to one another in relationships, specifically when the subject is money, a subject that pervades many aspects of life. Relationships are tough. Opportunities for differences and conflict abound, from child rearing to sex to recapping the toothpaste, but money issues can set off some of the largest fireworks (and produce plenty of smoldering hot spots just under the surface) in a relationship. This chapter covers common money problems couples face, how those problems manifest themselves, and how to solve them. Specifically, I will address:

- handling money issues during courtship, including prenuptial agreements,
- advice for how to manage money harmoniously as a couple, and

- dealing with divorce and the financial issues relating to splitting up.

Couples and Money

If couples don't disagree and fight about money, at least occasionally, it's probably because they don't talk about the subject at all rather than because they're always in agreement on financial issues. Howard Markman, director of the Center for Marital and Family Studies at the University of Denver and coauthor of *Fighting for Your Marriage* (Jossey-Bass) says that money is the number-one problem that couples fight about (more on why this is the case in the next section).

Andy and Joanne's marriage was, in many ways, a classic example of opposites attracting. The differences extended into many facets of their lives and often seemed to strengthen their bond, but when it came to money, the differences created conflict. Joanne loved saving it, while Andy enjoyed spending it. Joanne clipped coupons, rarely treated herself to any indulgences, and took great pride in saving the maximum in her retirement plans. Andy, meanwhile, spent lots of money on his hobbies, motorcycles and sports, and occasionally accumulated credit card debt due to overspending.

The friction and fights grew over the years, as did the insults. On one particular day in my office, Joanne fired the first salvo, "You spend irresponsibly and only think of yourself!" which prompted Andy to retort, "You may die with more money, but you don't know how to have fun and enjoy life!" Like many couples, they frequently had the same fights over the same issues.

Fortunately, over the years of working with them, I helped Andy and Joanne grow to realize that they must compromise and be more accepting of the other's differing money personality. They instituted a budget and spending limit for Andy that allowed him to spend a modest amount as he chose, while he also began a regular savings program. Joanne agreed to save a little less money than she had before and splurge from time to time.

Why Couples Fight about Money

Almost without exception, when I ask couples to recount their dating days, it's clear that they rarely, if ever, seriously talked about money issues. Most people are raised to believe that it's impolite and inappropriate to discuss money with others—it's a private, personal, and confidential matter. Most couples in courtship are in denial about the importance of all things financial, even though it's a huge issue looming on the horizon for the relationship.

Marriage takes place, the couple enjoys a honeymoon period when all is right with the world and their relationship, and then, over time, personality differences relating to personal financial management slowly emerge and cause friction. Although arguments and disagreements about money often stem from other broader relationship issues, the communication that does take place typically fails to improve the situation. "Couples get locked into accusatory, judgmental patterns of conversing with one another. In order to handle money well, couples need to communicate, negotiate and compromise," says divorce attorney Violet Woodhouse, author of *Divorce and Money* (Nolo Press).

I've long been fascinated about the differences between men and women and how they think about and relate to each other regarding money. A lot has been written about gender differences and money, but much of it is, frankly, dopey and not empirical or based on research. Consider, for example, some of these gems, which come from a leading financial magazine quiz titled "Do You Manage Your Money Like a Boy or Girl?"

The question: You buy a lottery ticket and win $2,000. Most likely, you use the windfall to:

A. put money in your kid's college fund,
B. pay bills, or
C. buy yourself an expensive present.

Option A is considered the female response, whereas option B is deemed the male response. Choice C is the gender-neutral answer.

The question: A grandparent recently died and left you a valuable watch. You:

A. sell the watch and invest the money,
B. wear the watch, or
C. put it in a drawer as a keepsake.

Option A was deemed the male response, option C the female response; B was the gender-neutral reply.

In my years of work as a financial counselor and columnist, I had many interactions with couples as well as opportunities to collect information from them. I can confidently make some generalizations about how men and women differ in relating to money in relationships, but please remember that these are simply generalizations, not hard-and-fast statements that apply to everyone.

For sure, women, as a group, are far more likely to ask for help and admit gaps in their knowledge than are men. I saw this tendency repeatedly in my work with couples. Men's egos more often get in the way of seeking assistance and education. Men are much more likely to plow ahead, even when they lack sufficient information and background on a money topic. My psychologist friends tell me that men, in our society, are more conditioned to view asking for help as a sign of weakness.

When it comes to investing, men are more willing to take risks. Although they may get themselves into trouble by relying too heavily on the investment vehicles that occupy the highest ends of the risk-return spectrum or leveraging themselves with borrowed money, for example, men are more likely to take the necessary risks to generate healthy long-term returns. However, as I cited in Chapter 4, researchers have found that men actually earn lower long-term returns than do women because men tend to trade too much. Though women may tend to be more conservative in their investment decisions, they do well long-term because they are far more likely to do their homework to find and then hold on to good investments.

Generational issues and trends play a role in explaining common financial differences between men and women. Prior to the rise of the feminist movement, many women were raised to view managing money as a man's job and with the belief that being financially dependent on a man was the default state of affairs. In more recent generations, women have generally been raised to think and act independently, including taking responsibility for making financial decisions. Men and women are both more apt to view a marriage as a true partnership between equals, which certainly has many benefits.

PRENUPTIAL AGREEMENTS: PROTECTION OR PROVOCATION?

Men and women who enter marriage with significant assets sometimes are concerned about protecting those assets for themselves and other family members, especially if they have children from a prior relationship. Enter the prenuptial agreement, a legal document that spells out who gets what in the event of divorce. Think of it as planning a financial divorce before you even get married.

Although it may seem painfully obvious, you'd be surprised by the number of people who overlook the fact that prenuptial agreements are an extremely sensitive topic to bring up. If you're considering broaching the topic, I can't stress the importance of the timing and approach enough. I've witnessed some engagements broken off as a result of proposed prenuptial agreements. That said, many more couples successfully navigate these tricky waters.

The first commonsense piece of advice I can offer you on this topic is to not spring the discussion or proposed agreement on your partner at the eleventh hour. In fact, a prenuptial signed too close to a wedding (for example, the day before the wedding) may not stand up to legal challenges if the argument can be made that the other spouse felt pressured into signing for fear of the wedding being called off at the last minute.

Bring up the topic as many months in advance of the proposed wedding date as possible. In fact, I wouldn't do any wedding planning at all until the topic is discussed and harmoniously resolved. Otherwise, you run the risk of having to call off a wedding should the agreement provoke problems. Schedule time to discuss the subject. Don't just bring it up out of the blue or, even worse, during a time of conflict. Each party should have his or her own attorney for review and counsel concerning the legal agreement. Last but not least, be sure to fully disclose your financial situation so that the agreement holds up legally.

Ultimately, the best reason to have a prenuptial agreement is being realistic and understanding that people change. Just because your fiancée verbally states that she doesn't want any of your money (or home equity, or portfolio, or . . .) as you stare lovingly into each other's eyes on a warm moonlit evening two months before your marriage doesn't guarantee that's how she will behave in a lawyer's office in the thick of an emotional divorce. As Dr. Phil McGraw says, "You marry one person but divorce a different one."

If you'd like to learn more about prenuptial agreements before meeting with an attorney, I recommend the book *Prenuptial Agreements: How to Write a Fair and Lasting Contract* by Katherine Stoner, attorney-mediator, and Shae Irving, JD (Nolo Press).

However, at least one downside to this leveling of the playing field exists: there is more *competition* within couples and marriages over money (among other issues). "There is far less 'we' thinking going on with couples today and far more 'me' thinking," says Woodhouse.

Achieving Financial Harmony as a Couple

As I discussed earlier, couples rarely delve into their financial philosophies and differences during their courtship and during the honeymoon phase of their relationship. Then, as problems and tensions arise and busy work schedules and other commitments get in the way of communication, issues fester and tend to worsen. That's why a little preventative maintenance can help. If you're currently in what looks to be a long-term relationship, don't keep putting money talks on the back burner. Take the risk to discuss your feelings, attitudes, and beliefs about money and be ready to respectfully listen to your partner's approach. More important than seeking a multipage written agreement to specify how you will handle everything, work at understanding your differences and decide on a process for negotiating agreements when conflicts inevitably arise. This will help minimize small problems mushrooming into big ones but, of course, doesn't guarantee a lifetime of trouble-free financial bliss.

Regardless of what point in your relationship, or whether, tension and disagreements have surfaced, it's vital to schedule a good time to talk. Talks should always be private and out of earshot of children, relatives, friends, and others.

When discussion is needed to resolve a problem, it helps not only to talk about concerns but also to share compliments, especially before you get to the issues you'd like to see changed. When concerns are raised, you dramatically increase the likelihood of your partner hearing, listening to, and respecting your point of view if you present it as your feelings on a topic rather than a criticism of the other person's financial habits. For example, instead of introducing a point of contention with "You're a reckless overspender," phrase the issue as "I'm concerned about having enough saved for retirement so that I don't feel chained to my job." Try "I'm really stressed that we haven't been saving enough to buy a home. Having a place of our own is important to me. Can we talk about it?" not "It's time for you to grow up and act like a responsible adult."

No matter what the topic is that you're at odds over, acknowledging, respecting, and even appreciating your partner's money-personality differences from yours is vital. Try to think openly about the situation for a minute. If you're a miser, be grateful if you didn't marry another miser. If you'd married another miser, you'd likely never enjoy the fruits of your hard work. Yes, a miser-spender marriage may produce fireworks on financial issues, but with open minds and open communication, such a pairing can also produce positive results, as both partners move away from their extreme polar behaviors to a more balanced and fulfilling position. Misers can learn that they can spend some money "frivolously," enjoy the experience, and not end up in financial ruin. Chronic overspenders can experience how good the sense of financial security feels that accompanies living more within one's means, paying down consumer debt, and beginning to see growing investment balances.

This give-and-take process and emphasis on compromise also works, of course, when other financial differences come into play. An aggressive, risk-loving investor paired with a conservative bank-account-loving partner can agree to take some reasonable and calculated risks with some of the money and be more careful with the rest of it. The root of successfully and happily managing money as a couple is compromise. You must remember that there's not just one "right" answer.

Also, realize that conflict over money issues happens, and constructively deal with it. Disagreements and differing points of view shouldn't be buried or viewed as a sign that your relationship is doomed or abnormal. Also, it's not healthy for one person to simply suck it up and give in all the time to their partner (building up resentment along the way). I've seen numerous couples in which divergent points of view were simply ignored, including one particular pairing of a spender and miser. The miser woman in one relationship kept plenty of her own money separate from the spender, but the spender husband was able to spend excessively using credit cards and other forms of consumer debt. As a result, the problems and differences didn't get addressed, while the debt balances grew and grew to dangerous levels. The reality of the situation wasn't acknowledged and confronted until I sat with the couple in my office and went through their assets and liabilities and showed them how little net worth was left due to the debts that were piling up. They had ignored the issue and, frankly, were in denial about it. It actually took me several meetings to get them to accept the reality of the situation.

I then helped them come to an agreement by focusing them on their shared goal of saving for retirement. They agreed to save about 12 percent of their incomes in tax-sheltered retirement accounts. The harder issue for the couple to deal with was what to do about the consumer debt the husband had amassed. The wife agreed to pay off about half of it because a sizable portion of the spending went toward the couple's home expenses and purchases. The husband agreed to cut up the credit cards and pay down the other half of the debt, a task that was accomplished within about eighteen months (the couple delayed saving the 12 percent monthly until all the consumer debt was gone).

All couples have plenty of financial tasks to take care of, so encourage open communication and shared responsibilities, while taking advantage of each partner's talents by matching tasks based on interests and skills. Start by developing a list of tasks and responsibilities, such as paying bills, shopping for and managing insurance issues, handling investments, and so on. Decide who will take care of each task, the level of consultation you're both comfortable with for that task, and how often the task will be performed. Put it all on paper so that you both know who's supposed to do what and when and to minimize the potential for misunderstandings down the road.

In addition to divvying up financial responsibilities, all couples should actively decide whether to keep money in separate or joint accounts or some of both. I'm not a fan of "his versus hers" money and completely separate accounts. (If you've been divorced and are getting remarried, you might consider a prenuptial agreement, which is covered in a sidebar earlier in this chapter, as an alternative.) Marriage is a partnership, after all, and, legally, state divorce laws generally treat a married couple's assets as pooled and divide them up upon divorce accordingly, even when they're in separately titled accounts. For many couples, pooling and sharing of accounts works fine, especially when communication is open and problems are productively addressed. Separate accounts and finances often create friction, especially if one person cuts back on work outside the home to be with the kids or if wide pay differences exist between the partners. I've also observed a tendency toward increased secrecy and related problems with separate accounts if spouses keep much of their spending habits

HIDING MONEY FROM YOUR SPOUSE

I've been surprised over the years by how many people have hidden stashes of money from their spouses. I first encountered this issue early in my career as a financial counselor when a physician client, who never met me with his wife present, volunteered the fact that he had hidden accounts. He justified hiding money from his wife by saying that "she has a wooden head."

If you think that your spouse does have a wooden head, hiding money isn't likely to be the best strategy! Many people fail to think about the implications should they unexpectedly pass away and how their surviving spouse would handle finances in such a case. The surviving spouse needs to know where to find important financial documents (investments, insurance, and so on), how to understand all of the arrangements, and how to handle matters going forward. Your spouse certainly won't be able to handle these responsibilities if assets are hidden and you don't discuss the details of your household's financial situation.

Worse-case scenario aside, the broader issue of marital trust comes into play. When I've pressed clients on why they hide assets, more often than not the reasons boil down to an overall lack of trust within the marriage that needs addressing. Some version of the following explanations is common. With each, I've presented an alternative way to think about the situation that is both more constructive and ethical:

"I don't want my spouse to know how much we really have saved because then he or she will pressure or expect me to

spend more."   In many cases, I've found that education and knowledge about the amount of assets needed for goals the couple share, such as retirement, go a long way to helping both sides be more realistic and honest with one another.

"My spouse doesn't deserve what he or she will get if we divorce, so I'll take what I really deserve for myself by hiding assets."   The spouse from whom the assets are being hidden usually has an inkling that something is afoot, especially after the realities of a divorce are setting in. Divorce attorneys have a variety of ways of ferreting out assets, and judges have been known to financially penalize those who hide assets.

"I'm worried that my spouse will prevent me from accessing money during a divorce, so I need to have a stash of safety money to tide me over."   This is a harder one to reason with. The lack of marital trust embedded in such a mind-set should be dealt with first and foremost.

"I've cheated on taxes (or in some other way) and need to hide my money."   I once had a counseling client who was a waiter and had been paid "under the table" for years. He had tens of thousands of dollars in his apartment! He was terrified to place this money in any investment account out of fear that it would be a red flag for the IRS. I advised him to get his money invested and physically safe (a fire or theft would've left him without a nest egg) and to then start properly and legally filing his taxes. He was even more horrified to learn that his tax evasion could land him in jail, in addition to the huge accumulating penalties he faced.

private. That said, a combination of joint and separate accounts is a workable compromise for some couples. The key to making this arrangement work is setting a discretionary spending limit. For example, you must consult your spouse on purchases of more than say fifty or one hundred dollars.

When all else fails, you can turn to other sources for assistance. Unfortunately, in my financial-counseling experience, I've found that most therapists and marital counselors are ill-prepared to help with financial issues. (You may be able to find a competent and ethical financial adviser who also has expertise in the psychological realm dealing with couples.) If you do go in search of a couples counselor to help you navigate and mediate your money differences, here are some specific issues that I advise you to investigate and interview questions that I suggest you ask:

Professional experience.   How many years have you done couples counseling? What portion of your current practice is devoted to couples? You want a therapist who has plenty of expertise and experience dealing with couples, not someone who just dabbles in such work.

Personal experiences.   Are you happily married? For how long have you been married? Is this your first marriage? Do you have children? Some therapists may not care for these more personal questions, and some will get defensive. Such responses can be telling. Although I respect everyone's right to privacy, I think that all of these questions are inbounds. Getting to the issue of whether the counselor is able to practice what he or she preaches isn't "prying." If you want to work on resolving your marital differences, you need to know up front if you're dealing with a therapist who is on his or her fourth marriage.

Approach to money. Please describe your philosophy on money management. How do you resolve financial disagreements in your family? What techniques do you recommend to your clients? Asking these questions will help you determine if you and your prospective therapist are on the same wavelength and can communicate about such important issues.

There are a number of books on the market purporting to help couples improve their relationships. Although a few titles hone in on financial matters, most don't; they cover money along with other common issues that cause problems with couples. Among my favorite couples-book authors are:

Dr. Phil McGraw. The famous television psychologist who got his big break on the *Oprah* show has written numerous critically acclaimed books including *Relationship Rescue* (Hyperion) and a separate *Relationship Rescue Workbook.*

Dr. Leo Buscaglia. I first saw Dr. Buscaglia years ago when he made regular PBS appearances. Unfortunately, Dr. Buscaglia, who was a professor at the University of Southern California, died of a heart attack in 1998. However, you can still find his many excellent and inspirational books, such as *Living, Loving and Learning* (Ballantine Books) and *Loving Each Other: The Challenge of Human Relationships* (Ballantine Books), at bookstores, especially online retailers.

Dr. John Gottman. Dr. Gottman is a psychology professor who has extensively tracked and studied thousands of married couples. Among his many books are *The Seven Principles for Making Marriage Work* (Three Rivers Press), *Why Marriages Succeed or Fail* (Simon and Schuster), and *The Relationship Cure* (Three Rivers Press).

Divorce: One of Life's Biggest Financial and Emotional Headaches

Always the skeptic of certain statistics, I long doubted the by-now common claim that half of all marriages end in divorce. Surely, I thought, the percentage couldn't be that high. Unfortunately, a quick check of national statistics confirmed for me that, indeed, about one in two marriages ends in divorce. Although I don't particularly enjoy writing about the depressing turns that life takes, divorce is one subject, clearly, with which more than a few people have become acquainted. As such, many folks need to know about the financial ramifications of the dissolution of their household and have information available to make the process as painless and "cost-effective" as possible.

Money is intimately connected with divorce. Within the marriage, arguments over household finances can push the marriage to its breaking point or serve as a symptom of a larger set of conflicts and hostilities. During a divorce, couples often argue over how to equitably divide the assets. After the divorce, the newly single often find that they must adjust to a lower household income and reconfigure financial plans.

During divorce, spouses are often forced to undergo a crash course in personal finances and divorce law while trying to deal with one of the most emotionally charged and draining episodes an individual can face. In fact, according to the Holmes and Rahe Social Readjustment Scale, developed by Thomas Holmes and Richard Rahe, going through a divorce is one of life's most stressful events.

As difficult as it may be, perhaps the most important step that you can take to ensure a "financially successful" divorce is to consciously separate your financial issues from your legal issues and emotional struggles. Both your emotional well-being and financial well-being are important, but if you let your emotions interfere with the financial decisions that you must make in the process of a divorce, neither party "wins," as legal bills will wreak greater havoc with your finances and further fray your nerves.

Victoria Felton-Collins, who runs a money-management firm that specializes in serving the needs of people getting divorced, says that divorce does not have to be "messy and expensive." She cites the case of one couple that had $5 million in assets yet spent only $5,000 in legal fees. On the other end of the spectrum, a couple with assets of $100,000 spent a whopping $20,000 on legal fees. In another case documented in the *Washington Post,* developer Richard Kramer was ordered by pay more than $800,000 to help his wife pay *half* of her legal bills in divorce court. The Kramers weren't fighting over custody of the children. They were haggling solely over money (the fortune was estimated to be in the tens of millions of dollars). "The time spent in this litigation by all of the involved attorneys and the bills resulting from them are obscene. This is one divorce, and it is costing millions of dollars," stated the judge. By separating their emotional life from their financial life, a divorcing couple may very well be able to settle out of court. Felton-Collins says that few divorce participants are happy with what judges decide, whereas negotiated settlements are usually "more palatable." In order to fight the irrationality of emotions, paralysis, and that overwhelmed feeling, she advises that participants break down the big undertaking into small, manageable tasks.

THE EMOTIONAL TOLL OF DIVORCE ON MEN, WOMEN, AND CHILDREN

Everyone who goes through divorce suffers emotionally, especially in the short term. But a Yale University School of Medicine study found that divorce causes and leads to about three times as many cases of clinical depression in men as in women. The National Center for Health Statistics found that divorced white men have a three times higher suicide rate as married men. One of the explanations for these numbers is that women are more likely to seek help with emotional and psychological issues (and sooner) and to share their feelings with friends. Men, unfortunately, are more likely to turn to drugs and alcohol for solace and to overinvest at work and become workaholics.

Last but not least are the children, on whom divorce is often the hardest. A common source of conflict in marriages with children is parents fighting about differing parenting styles. It's sad to see parents sabotaging each other using their children and not putting the best interest of the child (which is being on the same page, whether married or divorced) first. Psychologists recommend that parents take classes on coparenting.

In addition to keeping your emotions at bay, educate yourself financially. I've found that many people report feeling less overwhelmed with the fallout from divorce and more empowered when they begin to improve their knowledge base. Sign up for a personal-finance course and pick up a few good books. You might also consider seeking financial advice, but be careful. Attorneys generally lack the training and related perspective to adequately analyze your entire financial picture. Most financial advisers sell products, not their time and service. Plus, most have little experience dealing with divorce-specific issues anyway. Consulting with a good tax adviser is worthwhile in some cases, as tax considerations weigh heavily in some divorce situations. For example, it's useful to know that payments for alimony are tax deductible, whereas payments for child support are not.

Planning for life financially postdivorce is also important. Most divorced folks are faced with lower incomes and higher costs of living. The main reason? Living together as a family is usually cheaper per person than maintaining separate households. One of the most important exercises for soon-to-be divorced individuals is to analyze their individual spending. Lower-income-earning spouses, who are typically women, face the biggest reduction in standard of living postdivorce. Your "new" budget will help justify requests for alimony or child support during the divorce and serve as a guide to adjust to a new financial life after the divorce. Other financial issues must be rethought as well after divorce. For example, your insurance needs may change, you may need to consider revising your retirement plan, and you may want to alter your investment strategy.

If you're not committed to divorcing, perhaps all this talk of consulting lawyers and transforming yourself into a financial and tax expert is daunting. To a certain extent, I say "good." I'm not being callous. Especially when minor children are involved, work at your marriage so that you can keep both halves of the whole intact. Consider seeking help from the resources I recommend earlier in this chapter as well as from a marriage counselor or psychologist if you just can't talk things out yourselves.

AFFAIRS MAKE MARRIAGE PROBLEMS WORSE

Without a doubt, one of the dumbest and most destructive things that a spouse can do is have an extramarital affair. Though the cheating spouse often attempts to justify the situation due to a lack of satisfaction with his or her partner, affairs do nothing but create further emotional turmoil for all parties involved. In addition to emotional scars, affairs can lead to sexually transmitted diseases, including HIV/AIDS, and siphon off family financial resources. Psychologists who are experts on the topic generally agree that having an affair is a choice. Rather than finding a productive way to work on relationship problems, the decision to have an affair is akin to running away from one's marital problems as the solution.

Those who have affairs and end them often have additional affairs in the future. In one survey of married people, a whopping 42 percent of women and 48 percent of men who had had affairs said they would do so again. And don't think that you'll find a loving, lasting relationship in an affair. "Relationships born out of affairs survive less than 5 percent of the time. If he'll do it with you, he'll do it to you. If he's living this deception with you today, how could you ever trust him if you did get into a legitimate relationship with him?" queries Dr. Phil McGraw.

I'm not aware of any married couple that hasn't been through some tough times. Having a good marriage takes work, perspective, and maturity to see that storms and challenges shall pass. When it seems that the going has gotten too tough, find a productive way to improve your marriage. Read some good self-help books. Find a competent and affordable marriage counselor. But don't have an affair.

RAISING
MONEY-SMART KIDS

I have to chuckle at the frenzy that takes places these days over college admissions, especially among parents and kids who have their sights set on the so-called competitive, or top, schools. In a misguided effort to produce superchildren with a list of activities that will put the other contenders to shame, kids have adultlike schedules now. At one time, this mania was confined to high school, but now it's trickling down to the middle school (and even elementary school) years, especially in more affluent communities. The kids aren't the only ones who are feeling the effects. Some parents, and their nannies, create full-time jobs for themselves reviewing and selecting extracurricular programs, completing enrollment materials, and shuttling kids back and forth for lessons, extra classes, personal tutors, you name it.

My parents, who never had the benefit of a college degree, did okay in raising three kids who all successfully completed Ivy League educations, went out into the world, and did well in our chosen fields. No one walks for more than an hour to school in three feet of snow in this story, but I do believe that the perspective my parents brought to raising us kids is informative: Our lives never revolved around a set of activities chosen by our parents to look good on a college application. Instead, they let us focus on being kids and prepared us for the future by instilling life lessons, some of which centered on the subject of sound financial management and responsibility. I played baseball growing up, ran track in high school, and worked. My siblings and I were far from overscheduled as kids. Most days, we were free to just be kids in our neighborhood. We also all learned how to handle money and make sound financial decisions with our parents' help. They taught us financial responsibility through various real-life activities and situations and encouraged us all to work part-time jobs that taught us even more about finances and the realities of the real world.

I conduct alumni interviews for Yale University, and I see plenty of kids with multipage activity schedules and extracurricular "accomplishments" who don't have a clue about what real life is like. Kids who've been insulated from the real world by taking part in a zillion activities invariably get rejected from the top schools and for good reason. These young men and women often lack passion (for something other than getting into a top school) and suffer from fatigue due to their packed schedules. They also usually don't know what a family budget looks like, what common investments are, or why and how to save for the future. They've gone through the motions of schedule-packed days in the misinformed hope of getting into a top college, but they (and their parents) were operating under the terrible misperception about what it takes to get into a top school. They also don't often think about or realize that they may be chasing something that isn't going to provide them with any significant long-term happiness or "success" in the real world.

If you don't teach your kids about the realities and issues surrounding money and personal-finance decisions, you're setting them up for unnecessary and easily avoidable problems when they go out into the real world. So, in this chapter, I'll help you navigate the role money plays in parent-child relationships and understand how to raise money-smart kids. The bulk of this chapter is devoted to specific action-oriented steps that you can take to properly teach your kids about personal finance. I also cover the prickly topic of inheritances and how to best be a giver and recipient.

What Kids Don't Learn about Money

As a parent, I know about the responsibilities and challenges of raising kids. I'm also well aware of the time crunch that many families deal with. Parents are busy. Kids are busy. Parents work—a lot. Kids go school, and when they aren't in school, they play sports, practice musical instruments, attend religious education, play video games and watch television, and participate in other activities. Too many have too much on their plates and not enough time to enjoy and finish it.

Although most of the parents I know want their children to have the best education possible and give reasonable thought and effort to teaching their kids various real-world skills, most parents whom I know also neglect to educate their kids about personal-financial matters. I don't think this is a conscious decision. In the rush of day-to-day life, most folks probably don't even think about the issue. In addition, many parents may not understand or know how to teach personal finance, or they may have their own problems and issues with the topic.

Some parents assume that personal-financial skills are covered in school, but that assumption is wrong. Schools are increasingly incorporating money issues into the existing curriculum (for instance, in math lessons), yet the broader concepts of personal-financial management still aren't taught in the vast majority of schools. When schools do attempt to touch on such issues, many (especially budget-strapped schools) rely far too heavily on "free" "educational" materials from the likes of VISA and MasterCard. These credit card titans provide lessons that implicitly and explicitly support carrying consumer debt (on credit cards, auto loans, and the like) as a sound way to finance significant purchases and living expenses. In fact, VISA and MasterCard school-supplied resources endorse spending upwards of 15 to 20 percent of one's monthly take-home income to pay credit card and other consumer debts!

Advertising Fills the Void

In the absence of a sufficient financial education, kids are still "learning" about scores of product-buying opportunities on a daily basis from the many marketers and purveyors of popular culture who are more than happy to partially fill the void (think Pokemon's "Gotta Get 'Em All" advertising campaign). They also learn lessons from the examples that we set as parents in relation to money. I say "partially" because (surprise, surprise) advertisers only teach children to value their products. Without parental involvement, children rarely learn how to thoughtfully spend, save, and invest money.

According to the American Academy of Pediatrics, the average American child sees about 40,000 commercials per year. Companies spend gobs of money promoting their products and brands to kids for one simple reason: it works. Kids can hum and sing along with commercial jingles at startlingly early ages. By first grade, children easily recognize many companies' advertising logos and brand names. Kids' preferences drive billions of dollars of spending, both their own purchases and, more important, their parents' buying decisions. You won't, for example, find most seven year olds wandering the aisles of a toy store looking for an educational building toy produced by a small manufacturer, but you will find them seeking out the newest version of Lego brand building blocks.

It's no wonder, then, that coupled with the lack of parental initiative and school-based personal-financial education for children, kids today know all too well how to borrow and spend but know little about investing and saving. According to a survey by the Jump Start Coalition, only 14 percent of high school seniors knew that stocks provide better long-term returns than bonds or savings accounts. Amazingly, one in seven of those seeking credit-counseling help is a college student. This latter figure is less shocking and more understandable when you consider that one in three college students has four or more credit cards and that many colleges and universities today receive hundreds of thousands to millions annually from credit card companies for on-campus promotion access.

The Results of Overindulging Children

As I'm sure you're well aware, children learn from the example we set as parents, both in words and in actions. Although it's bad enough that our kids are bombarded with promotions and temptations to spend their money, some parents exacerbate that problem by acquiescing to too many requests and demands that their children make. This reinforces a mind-set focused on spending and consumption to the detriment of saving and investing. In my observations, some parents overindulge their children and fail to set limits for the following reasons:

Peer pressure. In this case, I'm actually talking about two kinds of peer pressure. For the parents, peer pressure comes in the time-honored tradition of keeping up with the Joneses by outfitting the family with all the "necessary" trappings of success. On the kid front, little Tyler and Brittany beg for all of the things that their classmates have.

Guilt. Parents who feel guilty about not spending more time with their kids tend to overschedule their children in after-school and weekend activities and provide them with the latest in everything. As I mention in Chapter 4, this pattern of indulgence often occurs when parents put in too much time at the office.

Detachment. Some parents simply don't want to be that involved in raising their kids. If they also face a time crunch due to work, overscheduling their kids is an easy solution.

Misguided thinking. Looking ahead to the competitive college admissions process, some parents believe they're enhancing their kids' chances of getting into Prestige U by enrolling them in two sports per season, along with chess, knitting, and math classes.

Ease of use. Setting and enforcing limits with kids are rarely easy and sometimes stressful. Some permissive parents find it easier, especially in the short term, to just give in to their child's demands.

William Damon, a professor of education and director of the Center on Adolescence at Stanford University, has reviewed and compiled the results of many studies that examined indulging children. These studies tracked kids into adulthood. Damon found that, when given too much too soon, indulged kids grow up into adults who have difficulty coping with life's disappointments and end up with a distorted sense of entitlement that gets in the way of success at work and in personal relationships. He also found that indulging children causes them to grow up into adults with a more egocentric, self-centered perspective, which raises mental health risks for depression and anxiety and greater risks for alcohol and substance abuse.

A Legacy of Financial Illiteracy and Bad Habits

While working with clients and answering questions from many readers, it has become clear to me that personal-financial habits are largely formed during childhood, and those habits that we adopt often mirror the financial practices of our parents. Although some children reject the examples that their parents provide, far more often, kids mirror the personal-financial habits they observe and experience at home. Adults who live it up now, borrow on credit cards and auto loans, and don't save for the future tend to raise children who are accomplished spenders and poor savers. The good news is that, often, the opposite is true as well. By setting a solid example of financial responsibility and providing a proactive financial education, you can supply your children with the necessary tools for financial success in the future.

Teaching Kids about Money

One of the great challenges in raising kids among our country's relative economic abundance is fulfilling the natural parental desire to provide children with opportunities for personal growth and development without spoiling them into dependency.

Striking a Balance between Spending Money and Spending Time

As I've already discussed earlier in this chapter, regularly overindulging kids can result in long-term damage to their emotional well-being, but you don't want to deprive them either. Suppose your daughter seems to have a talent and passion for music. Should you not enroll her in music classes or get her private lessons outside of school simply because doing so may seem extravagant—especially if you didn't grow up with such opportunities? And where do you draw the line with such expenditures, especially when money is tight or you and your spouse have different philosophies and beliefs about such spending?

Of course, you should provide for your kids. The great danger, especially in more affluent families or in less affluent families willing to spend beyond their means, is engaging in continuous and excessive spending on our kids with the implicit belief that more is better. Being a good parent requires some hard work. Although saying yes is more fun and makes you more popular, especially in the short term, psychologists universally agree on the importance of setting limits and saying no. Explaining and enforcing limits create feelings of security for children and actually demonstrate to them that you care. And it teaches them that, indeed, money doesn't grow on trees or come in unlimited supplies from credit cards. Kids benefit immensely from learning to work for things—saving, making choices, sacrificing, and contributing to their families and households through chores. After all, isn't that what the real world is all about?

I talked earlier in the chapter about the reasons parents indulge their children. I've observed that parents who buy too much for their kids have difficulty changing that habit. The key is to learn new ways to show that you love and care for your children rather than buying so much. Here are some ideas. They may seem like no-brainers when you read them, but the challenge is actually following through on the suggestions:

Rededicate yourself to hugs and kisses. The busier we get, the less affection we tend to give our kids. Like work, raising children can become a series of tasks to accomplish, activities to complete, and deadlines to meet—without us even noticing the change. We can all benefit by slowing down and sharing affection with our kids.

Play a game together. Here's a warning: after you make the decision to spend some time playing games with your kids, you may have to free up their time and, quite honestly, provide some "encouragement" to win them over to the idea. To facilitate the process, it helps to have "electronic-free days" in your home. In our family, we set aside two weekdays each week when there's no television, computer, or video games (in addition to the time-usage restrictions in place on other days). We imposed this digital moratorium to make time for other things that were increasingly being crowded out.

Go for a walk and talk.   Many kids will resist, but taking a walk with one of your kids can be a great way to get some fresh air and exercise while taking a few minutes to connect and have fun. Just try not to have unrealistic expectations for lengthy, deep, and profound conversations. Just take a walk and see what happens.

Catch them doing something good.   In many parents' efforts to teach their children good habits and extinguish poor practices, we can focus too much on correcting the negative. Praise and compliments increasingly get crowded out and overlooked. Don't let that happen in your family—catch your child doing something well several times every day!

Get involved in their world.   Whether you build something, do an art project, or play catch in the yard, don't just be a spectator. Get down and dirty, have some fun, and enjoy being a kid again! All those to-do lists around the house and at work that keep you from lending a hand or joining the fun more often will always be there waiting for you, but, before you know it, your kids will be grown and out of the house.

Go out for a meal with one child.   Okay, so this one does involve some spending. However, many parents find that, when they think about it, they don't have much one-on-one time with individual kids, especially in families with multiple children. So, periodically grab lunch or dinner with one of the kids.

Understand the Value of Personal-Financial Education

According to a survey conducted by the National Bureau for Economic Research, children who get personal-financial education in high school save 5 percent more of their incomes than kids who aren't exposed to such education. Five percent may not sound like a lot, but, when you consider that most adults should be saving about 10 percent annually to accomplish their financial goals and actually save less, a 5 percent difference is huge.

Although high school is a terrific time to teach kids key personal-financial concepts before they're nudged out of the family nest, you can and should begin to teach kids about money much sooner. The elementary school years, when kids are learning math concepts and getting comfortable with numbers, are an excellent time to lay a solid knowledge base. And, as opposed to teenagers, young children are generally more interested in listening to and learning from parents and other adults in their lives.

Starting with an Allowance

An allowance is an exceptional way to introduce children to a whole host of personal-financial lessons. In fact, a well-implemented allowance program can mimic many money matters that adults face every day throughout their lives. From recognizing the need to earn the green stuff to learning how to responsibly and intelligently spend, save, and invest their allowance, children can gain a solid financial footing from a young age.

Consider beginning a regular allowance when your kids reach the five-to-seven age range, around the time that a child is learning to read and master basic math skills like simple addition and subtraction. As for a dollar amount, consider a weekly allowance of fifty cents to one dollar per year of age. So, for example, a six-year-old child would earn between three and six dollars per week. Of course, the size of the allowance should depend, in part, on what sorts of expenditures and savings you expect your child to engage in and, perhaps, the amount of "work" you expect your child to perform around the house.

I believe that allowances should be earned—children shouldn't just get one for "showing up." The tasks required of them to earn the allowance can vary. For younger children, they can be as simple as what I was expected to do as a kid— making my bed daily and carrying my dishes from the table after a meal. As kids grow older, you can assign other household chores, such as cleaning their room, taking care of the family pets, or mowing the lawn. This approach demonstrates that additional responsibilities and harder work are often accompanied by additional rewards. Also, if you have children close in age, consider rotating the various tasks to keep things interesting and avoid all "fairness"-based grievances from the younger set.

I advise parents to have their kids always save a significant portion (up to half) of their allowance money toward longer-term goals, such as college. The allowance system that I personally prefer is for children to reserve about one-third of their weekly take for savings.

After they've earmarked their savings money, you can take the opportunity to pass along the importance of charity to your kids. We have our kids put about 5 to 10 percent of their allowance into a box earmarked for charity. For example, when the tsunami hit Southeast Asia and Hurricane Katrina battered the Gulf Coast, they donated what they'd accumulated in the charity box (nearly fifty dollars) for victim relief.

The amount that can be spent should by and large go toward "discretionary" purchases, especially when kids are younger. You want kids to learn how to make purchasing decisions and learn from their mistakes, including running out of money until their next allowance payment if they overspend. (I don't agree with the philosophy of giving kids a larger allowance and then having them, for example, buy their school lunches and other required purchases with that money. Do you really want your eight year old to go hungry on Thursday and Friday because he spent too much earlier in the week?)

I've long cautioned my own kids about viewing all forms of advertising with a skeptical eye, but a single purchasing decision provided a more powerful lesson for them than all my warnings and reminders combined when they ran into some used Pokemon cards on eBay. They thought they were getting the deal of a lifetime because they'd heard of single Pokemon cards being "worth" forty dollars, yet here they were buying dozens of cards for less than ten dollars! As I expected, they were quite disappointed with their purchase because they ended up with a bunch of mediocre cards that were likely "worth" less than they paid. (One obvious caution when allowing kids to make their own mistakes is that you need to be involved sufficiently to keep them from buying or accessing inappropriate items and material and to keep them from committing to a transaction that is more costly than they can afford. The Internet particularly problematic in this regard.)

For larger desired purchases, kids can leases over weeks of their weekly allowance earmarked for has a boy who and even months. For example, a far wanted a more expensive bike than his parents were willing to pay for. So the boy saved the extra seventy-five dollars he needed, and it took him nearly six months to accomplish his goal. Besides learning how to save toward a larger purchase and not getting in the bad habit of borrowing for consumption, this experience provided some additional benefits that surprised the parents. "I've never seen my son take such good care of a bike as the new one he bought partly with his own money," said his father.

As kids accumulate more significant savings as the weeks turn into months and the months turn into years, you can introduce the concept of investing. Rather than trekking down to the boring old local bank and putting the money into a sleepy low-interest bank account, I prefer having kids invest in mutual funds (which you can do through the mail or online). Although stocks returning an average of 10 percent per year sounds attractive to most grownups, young kids may not be able to comprehend what that kind of returns really means or the long-term power of compounding returns. I find that kids can better understand these mathematical concepts beginning in late elementary school when they're comfortable with more complicated multiplication. I have two useful ways to explain and illustrate to kids how small regular investments can grow into substantial amounts over time through modest returns from sound investments. One is to work out on paper how money grows over the years. The second approach is to show kids with play money.

Other Ways to Teach Kids about Money

Though allowances are an awesome way to teach kids about money, there are numerous other steps you can take to make your kids financially savvy. Among my favorites are:

Reduce their exposure to ads. The primary path to reduced exposure to ads is to cut down on TV time. When kids are in front of the tube, have them watch prerecorded material. You can direct the television viewing of younger children, in particular, toward videos and DVDs. And for older kids, if you use digital video recorders, such as TiVO, you can zap out the ads.

Teach your kids about the realities of advertising and marketing. Invest the necessary time to teach and explain to your kids that the point of advertising is to motivate consumers to buy the product by making it sound more wonderful or necessary than it really is. Also explain that advertising is costly and that the most heavily promoted and popular products include the cost of all that advertising, so they're paying for it when they buy those items.

Read good books on the topic with your child. The Berenstain Bears series has some terrific titles such as *The Berenstain Bears Get the Gimmies* (Random House Books for Young Readers). For late elementary school–age kids, *Quest for the Pillars of Wealth* by J. J. Pritchard (Lantern Press) is a chapter book that teaches the major personal-financial concepts through an engaging adventure story. Consumer Union, publishers of *Consumer Reports*, also publishes a kids magazine called *Zillions* that covers money and buying topics.

Play games that teach good money habits. Games that I've played with kids that I think are fun and teach proper financial habits include The Allowance Game, Monopoly, and Life.

Teach them how to shop wisely. Being a smart consumer requires doing your homework, especially when buying costly products. Teach your kids the value of product research (including using sources like *Consumer Reports* for product reviews) and comparison shopping. Demonstrate how to identify overpriced and shoddy merchandise. Finally, show them how to voice a complaint when returning defective products and go to bat for better treatment in service environments, two additional tasks that are part of being a savvy consumer.

Introduce the right and wrong ways to use credit and debit cards. Those plastic cards in your wallet offer a convenient way to conduct purchases in stores, by phone, and over the Internet. However, credit cards, unfortunately, offer temptation for overspending and carrying debt from month to month. Teach your kids how a checking account works, explaining that debit cards are connected to your checking account and thus prevent you from grossly overspending as you easily can on a credit card.

Be mindful of your statements and attitudes about money. Kids are little sponges. They learn a lot from what you say and how you say it and your actions. Do you encourage shopping or gambling as a form of recreation and entertainment? If you're critical or judgmental of people with money, your kids may learn envy or that having money is somehow wrong.

Encourage them to get a job. Your child's initial exposure to the work-for-pay world can start with something as simple as a lemonade stand. I had an extensive newspaper route for a number of years, and I cut lawns and did other yard work during high school and college summers. By holding down such jobs, kids learn about working, earning, saving, and investing money. It provides welcome relief for parents to not continually be

PLANTING THE ENTREPRENEURIAL SEED

As I've discussed, there are lots of good lessons that can come from having children doing some work. I enjoyed earning money through various jobs as a kid. Having a paper route was a great source of pride and satisfaction. I learned a tremendous amount about the realities of the business world and good customer service. There's no doubt in my mind that my successes as an entrepreneur grew out of the lessons and abilities I learned at an early age. I "graduated" to running a lawn-cutting and yard-maintenance business throughout the summer during my high school and early college years. The lawn service taught me additional lessons about running a business and paid me substantially more than the fast-food jobs most of my peers had. (I lasted about one week as a dishwasher at the local Howard Johnson's restaurant, which was about six days longer than I should have stayed!)

A colleague of mine recently shared his childhood work experiences with me, and I think they further highlight the value of work-related experiences for kids.

When I was young, my dad wrote up contracts for me when I wanted something, like a new baseball glove. I would be paid modest amounts for various chores, and once I had accumulated enough for the item, we would go and buy it. Once a year, the town fair came, and I would get paid a penny for every dandelion that I pulled from the yard. I usually pulled 500 to 1,000 and had five or ten bucks to blow on rides and cotton candy at the fair.

> In about fifth grade, I realized that there was far better cash to be made outside the confines of my extortionist family! I began to hire myself out to the neighbors for shoveling snow and yard work. I took great pride in my work, and I loved being my own boss and setting my own schedule.

the source of spending money. Working outside the home does raise some safety issues. By all means, be involved in ensuring that your child has a safe work environment.

Passing Down Money: Estates and Inheritances

In my work as a financial counselor, I was often amazed at the dramas played out and the issues raised over the transfer of money and wealth between the generations when someone passed away. Inherited money almost always came with some strings attached. This important section will help you deal with this often prickly issue.

Retirees often worry about depleting their assets due to chronic health problems and either running out of money or not having anything left over for their heirs. These folks may be reluctant to enjoy their wealth in their golden years. However, most retirees don't end up with protracted nursing home stays, so people tend to die with more money than they anticipated. If you're currently considering such issues, you can determine the sufficiency of your assets and gain some peace of mind. T. Rowe Price has some excellent resources on their Web site (http://www.troweprice.com) and in printed booklets (1-800-638-5660) for helping determine if you have enough assets to support your desired lifestyle through retirement and have a bit left over for future generations, if that's your goal. Alternatively, you could engage the services of a good financial adviser.

Most parents prefer to pass along some wealth and associated financial security to their offspring. Problems come into play, though, when too much wealth may be passed along. John Levy, a "wealth counselor," says that expectations of a substantial inheritance can delay one's offspring from growing up and maturing. His advice to parents is to make sure that kids work growing up and postcollege, which leads to self-esteem, self-reliance, and independence. That's great advice.

To make sure that your kids get some money from your estate, but not too much, I recommend giving your money away gradually, while you're still alive. Especially if you have enough assets to know that your heirs will be receiving at least modest sums, consider giving away some money each year. You may give up to $11,000 (free of federal taxation) in assets to each of as many people as you desire annually. If you're married, your spouse may give an additional $11,000 per year. The advantage of giving money gradually is that you can see how your heirs are using (or abusing) their newfound wealth, a perspective that you obviously don't have if you wait to pass along your entire estate when you die.

Taking this approach does come with a few potential pitfalls to be aware of. It's the rare parent who is able to give money to their kids and say nothing about how they should or should not use or manage it. Offering some guidance and advice is fine and to be expected, but don't try to set restrictions. You did your best raising your kids, providing them with a fine education, and teaching them about life. Now you're providing them with an additional leg up in the world. Let them make the most of *their* opportunities and show you how much they've learned.

Likewise, don't use periodic distributions of your estate or the promise of an inheritance to get your kids or their spouses to do what you want them to do in other aspects of their lives (starting a family, moving closer to home, or buying a house, for example). If your son or daughter or his or her spouse has an addiction, that's another matter. In that case, I say withholding the money until the problem is properly addressed is a legitimate course of action.

INDEX

ABOUT THE AUTHOR

Eric Tyson is one of the nation's best-selling personal finance book authors and has penned five national best sellers (he is also the only author to have four of his books simultaneously on *Business Week*'s business book best-seller list). His *Personal Finance for Dummies* (Wiley) won the Benjamin Franklin Award for Best Business Book of the Year. He is also the author of *Investing for Dummies* and co-author of *Home Buying for Dummies* and *Real Estate Investing for Dummies*, among other titles.

Eric writes a syndicated newspaper column and is a former columnist and award-winning journalist for the San Francisco Examiner. His work has been featured and quoted in hundreds of local and national publications and media outlets including *Newsweek, The Wall Street Journal, Los Angeles Times, Chicago Tribune, Forbes, Kiplinger's Personal Finance, Money, Worth, Parenting,* and *USA Today*, as well as on NBC's *Today Show*, ABC, CNBC, PBS's *Nightly Business Report*, CNN, CBS national radio, NPR's *Sound Money*, and Bloomberg Business Radio. He was also a featured speaker at a White House conference on retirement planning.

Tired of working as a management consultant to Fortune 500 financial service firms that were more interested in maximizing short-term profits than in providing sound financial products and services, Eric founded, in 1990, the nation's first financial counseling firm that works exclusively on an hourly basis. He started his new company with a simple mission: to provide objective, cost-effective, personal financial advice, especially to nonwealthy Americans. Through family and friends, Eric had seen many intelligent people make horrendous mistakes in managing their money.

In addition to his writing and counseling, Eric also taught the nation's most highly attended personal financial management course at the University of California, Berkeley. A dynamic and provocative speaker, he has spoken at many corporations and nonprofits.

His educational background includes a bachelor's degree in economics from Yale and an MBA from the Stanford Graduate School of Business.